Equity Records

of

Old 96 &
Abbeville District,
South Carolina

Vol. #1

This volume was reproduced from
a 1957 edition located in the
Publishers's private library
Greenville, South Carolina

Please direct ALL correspondence and book orders to:
Southern Historical Press, Inc.
PO Box 1267
375 West Broad Street
Greenville, SC 29602-1267
www.southernhistoricalpress.com

Originally printed & copyrighted: Liberty, S.C.
Reprinted by: Southern Historical Press, Inc.
                            Greenvill, SC   29601
ISBN #0-89308-530-8
Printed in the United States of America

1

October 1957
Box 129
Liberty, S.C.

TO WHOM IT MAY CONCERN,

This is to certify that I, Pauline Young of Liberty, S.C.
(formerly of Abbeville, S.C.) do certify that the records
contained within this volume are copies I made from the originals
on file in The Abbeville Court House, they are my own compilation,
and not from any other persons. That these were copied from the
old Equity Records which I discovered in the Courthouse there, that
was saved from a fire back in 1875 I have been told. These records
along with the other records I found are being compiled into books
for the benefit of the people. A copy of this book has been placed
on file in the Clerk of Courts Office, Abbeville, S.C. for the use
of the public who may visit the courthouse there. To help protect
the original records. My work is recommended by Earl Nickles, Clerk
of Court in Abbeville, S.C. from whose office these records were
made from. Some of the records were so dim, and the writing was so
bad, it was impossible to make some of them out correctly. If you
come across a word with a question mark after it, you will know
that I was'nt postive of the word. I do hope that you will enjoy
this book and that it will be of some help to you in your research
work.

Yours sincerely,
Miss Pauline Young, Genealogist
Box 129, Liberty, S.C.

" DEDICATED TO A HANDFUL OF DUST."

COPYRIGHT 1957

ROBERT ANDERSON vs. JOSEPH COLHOUN
BILL FOR INJUNCTION
CLERK OF COURTS OFFICE, ABBEVILLE, S.C.

State of South Carolina
In the Court of Equity) To the Honorable John Matthews, Richard
Hutson, and Hugh Rutledge Esquires, Judges of the Court of Equity
of the State of South Carolina.

Humbly complaining sheweth unto your Honors, your orator
Robert Anderson of the County of Pendleton, in the District of
Washington, and State aforesaid Squire and your orator John Lin-
dsay of Wilkes County in the State of Georgia.

That some time in or about the year of our Lord, One thousand
seven hundred and (no date given here,P.Y.) the Legislature of
the State of Georgia, passed a Law, intitled an Act for inflicting
penalties on, and Confiscating the Estates of such persons, as
are therein declared guilty of Treason, and for other purposes
therein mentioned, and that certain Commissioners were by the
General Assembly of the said State chosen and elected to carry the
said Act of Confiscation and Banishment fully into effect, with
full powers to collect by their Agents or otherwise all property
by the said Act confiscated, which might be found in the State of
Georgia, or any other of the united States. As in and by the said
Act of the General Assembly of the said State of Georgia a copy
whereof now in the hands of your Orator, ready to be produced to
this Honourable Court may appear, and to a copy whereof here with
filed, your Orator begs leave to refer as often as occasion may
require. And your orator insists that the said Commissioners by
virtue of the powers in them vested did constitute and appoint
your orator of the State of Georgia Esquire, their sole Agent, for
collecting, and taking into his possession and charge, all the
property belonging to the said State of Georgia, consisting of
Negroes, Horses, and other property and effects, which had been
confiscated, as aforesaid, and which had been stolen from the persons comprehended in the said confiscation Law, or removed, or
carried away into the State of Virginia, or into North or South
Carolina, by an instrument of writing under their hands and Seals,
dated at Savannah in the said State of Georgia on the fourth day of
September in the year of our Lord one thousand seven hundred and
eighty two. Your orators further insists, that by the said instrument of writing, the said Commissioners fully empowered, and authorised the said John Lindsay to employ all lawfull ways and
means for effecting the said Agency and business, for the purpose
of haveing the property so removed, brought back into the said
State of Georgia, and delivering the same up to the said Commissioners, to be by them disposed of, agreeable to the directions of
the said Act, as in and by the said instrument of writing & other
Testimonials accompanying it, now in hands of your orator, ready
to be produced to this Honorable Court may appear, and to which
your Orator begs leave to refer as often as occasion may require.

Your Orators hath heard and believes it to be true, that several Negroes, and other property, claimed by or belonging to Joseph Colhoun Esquire(the Defendant hereinafter named) were by some person or persons then & still unknown to your Orators, plundered from him, some time during the late war, but your Orators insists that all, or most of the said Negroes, and other property, so plundered, from the said Joseph Colhoun as aforesaid, returned to their said claimant, or owner, or were by him collected and received. Your Orators Robert Anderson & John Lindsay charges and in sists, that in or about the month of September, in the year of our Lord, one thousand seven hundred and Eighty two, the said Joseph Colhoun in company with three armed Men , himself also being armed, went to the house of Samuel Red in the State of Georgia, where was three Negroes, Viz. Jane, Jude and Squire, a part of the undivided Estate of Thomas Loyd Senior, Deceased, late of the State of Georgia, and having taken the said Samuel Red a prisoner, was carry ing him against his willgly compulsion? and the said three Negroes to Colonel Elijah Clarke, of the State of Georgia, who was very inviterate, rigorous, and severe against Tories, and he the said Samuel Red being one of the people called Tories and threatened severely was glad to get released on any terms, and therefore after they arrived at the Colonels plantation, was forced, in order to obtain his liberty, to make a pretence of giving up the said three negroes, Jane, Jude and Squire aforesaid to the said Joseph Colhoun and his armed company as aforesaid. Your Orators hath also been informed and verily believes it to be true, that the said Samuel Red never owned, or claimed any part of the said three negroes, as his property, but the said Samuel Red, at the time the said Joseph Colhoun obtained the possession of the said three negroes happened to lodge with one of the Children of the said Thomas Loyd Senior deceased, with whom the said three Negroes lived. Your orators have been informed and believes it to be true, that the said Samuel Red was not the person that plundered any part of the property of the said Joseph Colhoun. That the said Samuel Red never was on the plantation of the said Joseph Colhoun during the late war, or since, and that the said Samuel Red never would have consented to the giving up of the said three Negroes, which did not belong to him, had it not been under fear and compulsion. That al though the said Samuel Red offered to give up to the said Joseph Colhoun, security to answer any demand, or charge, that the said Joseph Colhoun had against him the said Samuel Red, and particularly mentioned, that he the said Samuel Red would give to the said Joseph Colhoun Colonel McCoy, and Captain Joshua Inman as such, the said Joseph Colhoun refused to take any Security, from the said Samuel Red, but insisted, either to have the said three Negroes, from the said Samuel Red, or to carry him and them also, be fore the said Colonel Elijah Clarke, in order to have Marshall Law put in force against him. And your Orators further shew unto your Honours, that soon after the appointment your orator John Lindsay as Agent to the Commissioners of Confiscated Estates of the State of Georgia aforesaid, the said John Lindsay proceeded on the execution of his duty, and having received information that there

were three Negroes, called Jane, Jude, and Squire, in the possession of the said Joseph Colhoun, which (as your orator Robert
Anderson has been informed and verily believes to true) and as
your Orator John Lindsay positively charges did belong to the un
divided Estate of Thomas Loyd Senior deceased, who by his last
Will and Testament(after the death of his wife Patience an Executrix) did Will and Bequeath that all his personnal Estate, should
be equally divided between his children here after named Viz.
Elisabeth, Thomas, Samuel, Francis, James, Jane, and Patience, as
in and by a certified copy of the said Will, now in the hands of
your Orators ready to be produced to this Honourable Court, may
appear. Your orators also insists, that the said John Lindsay, was
fully authorised, and impowered, to sue for, recover, and bring
back, the said three Negroes, Jane, Jude and Squire, aforesaid in
behalf of the Female and minor Heirs of the undivided Estate of
Thomas Loyd Senior deceased, as aforesaid. Your orators further
insists, that the said three Negroes Jane, Jude and Squire were
deemed and considered as confiscated property to the State of
Georgia, as belonging to Thomas Loyd Junior, and Samuel Loyd, who
were known and declared enemies to the Country in the late War
with Great Britian, and very obnoxious characters, and whose property, by the said Act of Assembly your orator the said John Lindsay
was instructed and advised as he psoitively asserts & Robert Ander
son or comprehended in, the Confiscation Act & no doubt intestain
ed of their guilts informed and verily believes to be true, was
confiscated. That a short time afterwards, that is to say on or a
bout the Seventeenth day of October one thousand seven hundred
and eighty two, the said John Lindsay went to the house of the
said Joseph Colhoun, in whose possession he found the said three
Negroes, that the said John Lindsay with civility and politeness,
informed the said Joseph Colhoun, of his business, and produced
to him his Commission and authority, from the Commissioners of Con
fiscated Estates of Georgia, and desired the said Joseph Colhoun to
deliver to him the said John Lindsay, the said three Negroes, as
the right and property of the State of Georgia and of Female and
minor orphans, heirs of the Estate of Thomas Loyd Senior deceased.
That the said Joseph Colhoun on the said first application declin
ed delivering them up, alledging that he the said Joseph Colhoun,
had received them from one Samuel Red as security for the return
of property which had been plundered from him the said Joseph
Colhoun, by the said Samuel Red, but the said John Lindsay, reas-
oned with, and assured the said Joseph Colhoun, that the said
three Negroes were not the property of Samuel Red, and that he the
said Samuel Red had no right to dispose of them, but that they
were the right of the State of Georgia, as confiscated property,
or the right of the minor heirs of the Estate of Thomas Loyd deceased. That the said Joseph Colhoun after advising with some of his
friends, informed the said John Lindsaythat he might take the said
three Negroes, which the said John Lindsay accordingly received
from the said Joseph Colhoun, and gave to the said Joseph Colhoun
a receipt for them, as Agent to the Commissioners of Confiscated
Estates in the State of Georgia aforesaid, and as, and for, the
right and property of the said State. That immediately after the

said John Lindsay had received the said three Negroes from the
said Joseph Colhoun as aforesaid, he carried the said three Negroes to Augusta in the State of Georgia, in order to deliver them
up to the said Commissioners, when it happened that a Board of
Commissioners of confiscated property, could not immediately be
converred, in consequence of which, on the twenty first day of
October, one thousand seven hundred and eighty two, the said John
Lindsay wrote a Letter to Thomas Lewis Esquire, one of the Commissioners of Confiscated property in ht e said State, in the words
or figures following

"October 21st 1782 - Sir, I have brought three Negroes from
Captain Joseph Colhoun, of the Loyds property, Viz. Jane, Jude and
Squire, a boy of five or six years old, Jane's child; Jude is with
child. I expected the Commissioners in Augusta, but could not find
them, and as the Negroes Mistress and family live in your County,
several Gentlemen recommended to me, to have the Negroes there,
untill the Commissioners make a board, and dispose of them as they
may think proper, as the keeping of them in a strange family would
be precarious, as Jude is so great with child, and Jane's being
so nigh home might run away - I have thought it proper to deliver
them to Mrs. Cartledge, one of the family they were used to live
in, and take security for their being accountable when you may
call for them - I am, with respect, your most humble Servant

                                            John Lindsay

N.B. I am so far on my way to North Carolina and Virginia, you
will please take an account of the Negroes, and do as the Law dir-
ects, or the commissioners will Judge necessary -

                                            John Lindsay
To Thomas Lewis, Commissioner

     Your orators beg leave to insist, that the conduct of the said
John Lindsay on that occasion, was highly approved of by some of
the said commissioners of confiscated propertyof the State of
Georgia and particularly the said Thomas Lewis Esquire, who
wrote to the said John Lindsay, on the subject in the manner
following

     "Sir - I received your friendly letter wherein you mentioned
your being troubled about the Negroes you delivered to Mrs. Cartledge, and wrote to me concerning, which I am sorry for . You also
mention that some ungenerous aspersions were thrown out by Captain
Colhoun, concerning your conduct, but I remember I received your
letter shortly after it was wrote and thought you perfectly in the
line of your duty - I am Sir with respect, your friend and humble
Servant -
                                            Thomas Lewis

To John Lindsay Esquire"

As in and by the said several Letters, now in the hands of
your Orators ready to be produced to this Honourable Court may at
large appear marked F. G. and the said John Lindsay avers he had
no evil design or intention to injure the said Joseph Colhoun,
but acted under an impression of duty with no view of benefit to
himself & without receiving any of the said negroes to his own
use. Your orators beg leave further to shew unto your Honours,
that the said Joseph Colhoun did actually commence a Suit in Law
against your orator the said John Lindsay, setting forth in his
declaration. "That on the seventeenth day of October in the year
of our Lord one thousand seven hundred and eighty three, he the
said Joseph Colhoun was possessed of the said three negroes, Jane,
Jude, and Squire aforesaid, as of his own proper goods and cahtt-
les". As in and by the said proceedings now in the hands of your
orator, ready to be produced to this Honourable Court, may, and
will, more fully appear; and to a certified copy whereof, here
with filed, your orators begs leave to refer, as often as occasion may require. Marked H. But your Orators charge and insists
that the said Joseph Colhoun, had freely and voluntarily deliver
ed them up according to the direction of commissioners of Confiscated Estates, of the State of Georgia, and the said commissioners
had disposed of them as they thought proper, almost a year before
the said seventeenth of October, one thousand seven hundred and
eighty three. Your orators further insists that the said John
Lindsay never claimed any right to the said Negroes on his own
account, and that he never received any benefit or profit, arising
from the said Negroes, and never converted them or any part of
them, to his own use, neither directly , nor indirectly. And your
Orators further insists, that no Affidavit was ever made, or
Sworn to, by the said Joseph Colhoun in order to hold the said
John Lindsay to Bail, or any order made by any of the Judges of
the said Court, either at Chambers, or in Court, to hold the said
John Lindsay to Special Bail in the said action as appears by
paper. Your orators John Lindsay Robert Anderson begs leave, further
to shew unto your Honours, that at the Aprill Court,one thousand
seven hundred and eighty five, the said cause Colhoun against
Lindsey was refered to arbitration by a rule of Court, but the
arbitrators not agreeing, the cause was returned into Court, and
during the siting of the same Court, a Verdict for two hundred and
ten pounds, and costs of Suit, was found against the said John
Lindsey. Your orators must beg leave to observe that they are
totally at a loss to know on what legal or just ground the said
Joseph Colhoun obtained such a Verdict from the Jury against the
said John Lindsey, but your orators have been informed, that the
said Joseph Colhoun pretended, that in fact, Jane, Jude, and
Squire, the three Negroes aforesaid, were in reallity the right
and property of Samuel Red, and that the said Samuel Red, had
voluntarily, and of his own free will and accord, put the said
three Negroes into his, the said Joseph Colhoun's possession, as
security for the return of some property, which he the said Joseph Colhoun pretended, had been plundered from him in the late war,
by the said Samuel Red, that the said Joseph Colhoun also pretend

ed , that the said John Lindsay had claimed the said three Negroes, as having been the property of the said Samuel Red, and the said John Lindsay avered that the property of the said Samuel Red was confiscated, and of coyrse that he, the said John Lindsey had a right to sue for, recover, and take into his possession and charge, the said three Negroes, as Agent for the Commissioners of Confiscated Estates, of the State of Georgia, and in as much as the Estate of the said Samuel Red had not been confiscated, the said Joseph Colhoun pretended, that the said John Lindsey, by false pretentions had taken from him, the said Joseph Colhoun the said three Negroes, Jane, Jude, and Squire aforesaid, which he the said Joseph Colhoun pretended to hold as Security for the return of property, which he also pretended had been plundered from him as aforesaid. But your Orators further insists that that the said John Lindsey had prepared Testimony vouchers, Certificates, and affidavits, under the Seal of the State of Georgia, to prove his case and defence; as in & by the said Vouchers, Certificates & Affidavits may appear, Copies of some of which your orators has been able to procure & which are herewith filed, to which your orators begs leave to refer as often as occasion may require, by papers marked No. 1 No 2 No 3 No 4 No 5, but in as much as they were not deemed legal evidence, they were not suffered to be read at the trial of the said cause; that there being no other mode of examining witnesses living in a foreign State, it was utterly impossible under these circumstances, for the said John Lindsey to prove his particular case, as all his witnesses lived in the State of Georgia, and the said John Lindsey knew of no law, to compel witnesses to attend to give Evidence, in the Courts of this State, or even to examine them by Commission, where they lived without the limits of this State, by occasion of which the said John Lindsey was not enabled to make any defence, at the trial of the said cause. But your orators Robert Anderson and John Lindsey charges and insists, that the said Joseph Calhoun had no foundation in justice to commence any Suit or Action at Law, against the said John Lindsey, for the recovery of any Debt or Damage of, and from the said John Lindsey & could not possibly in their opinion & belief have obtained a verdict against him if the whole case is opposed by his Testimony had gone to the Jury. But the said Joseph Colhoun by Circumentation? Surprise and artful Contrivance procured a judgment at law againsty your orator Robert Anderson under pretext that your orator was Security for the said John Lindsey and the said Joseph Colhoun now pretends that your orator Robert Anderson is liable to pay him the amount of Judgment, being two hundred and thirty six pounds 18/4 — altho your orator insists Robert Anderson & John Lindsay and the truth is, that your orator Robert Anderson never did and act whereby he became or intended to become security, for the payment of any money for or on account of the said John Lindsey to the said Joseph Colhoun. In proof of which and to shew of what nature the unjust, and unreasonable demand, of the said Joseph Colhoun is your orators beg leave to shew unto your Honours, that some time in or about the month of Aprill, in the year of our Lord one thousand seven hundred and eighty four, your orator Robert Anderson

attending on his business, during the sitting of the Court at the
Village of Ninety Six, accidently happened in company with the
said John Lindsey, that the said John Lindsey, in conversation
with your orator Robert Anderson represented the situation of a
certain Suit, that was then depending, between the said Joseph
Colhoun, and the said John Lindsey, and observed to your Orator
Robert Anderson that the said action would not be tried during
the siting of that Court, but that, as he the said John Lindsey
lived in another State, the said Joseph Colhoun's Lawyer, Thomas
Pinckney Esquire informed him, that he must give security for his
personal appearance at the next ensuing Court; when the Action
would certainly be tried, and expressed some uneasiness at such
a request, as his friends had gone from Court; and the said John
Lindsey appeared by his conversation and manner of talking, as if
he wanted your orator Robert Anderson to become his Security for
that purpose. Your oratir Robert Anderson answered, that he your
Orator could rest the matter upon his the said John Lindseys own
honour, that he your Orator was sure that he the said John Lindsey
would not let his Securities suffer by with holding his personal
attendance at Court, upon his own business, and there fore offered
to the said John Lindsey, that if he the said John Lindsey would
get another person, he might name your Orator Robert Anderson as
one of his Securities, for his personal appearance at the next
ensueing Court. And your Orators further sheweth unto your Honors
that some time after, and on the evening of the same day in
which the conversation aforesaid had passed between your Orator,
and the said John Lindsey, when your orator Robert Anderson was
in a public house in the said Town of Ninety Six, and at the in-
stant when your orator was busily.engaged in writing the Deposition of a poor widow, your orator the said John Lindsey came into
the room where your orator Robert Anderson was writing the Deposition aforesaid, and in great haste told your orator, that he
the said John Lindsey had been long in quest of him, Lawyers
was in a great hurry, and said that if he your Orator would only
sign his name, on that piece of paper, Colonel Brandon would do
so likewise, and that would be sufficient; that your Orator Robt-
ert Anderson (seeing nothing but a piece of white paper lying be
fore him, with only yhe words"Entered paper, except the said word)
answered the said John Lindsey, what is on that blank paper? to
which the said John Lindsey replied, that was all the Lawyers
wanted, and they were in great haste; and your orator without
further inquiry , or examination, hastily signed his name on the
same paper, which your Orator solemnly declares, and protests, he
considered, and believed, as a mere assurance to the Lawyer who
was concerned for the said Joseph Colhoun, that the said John
Lindsey would make his personal appearance at the next ensueing
Court, to be holden at Ninety Six, and for no other use, intent,
or purpose whatsoever. And your Orator Robt Anderson further
sheweth unto your Honors, that immediately after he your Orator
had so subscribed his name, on the said piece of paper as afore
said, that the said John Lindsey left the room, where he found
your orator busily writing as aforesaid, and your Orator Robert
Anderson did not afterwards see the said John Lindsey, untill his

arival at Ninety Six, in November Court following, where your
Orator saw him the said John Lindsey attending on the said Court,
which made your Orator perfectly easy and satisfied, and from that
moment your orator always considered himself perfectly released,
and discharged from any engagement he had made, by an offer to
become the said John Lindsey's Security, for his personal appearance at the Court, or by his signing his name on the piece of
paper as aforesaid, and consequently your orator Robert Anderson
gave himself no further trouble or concern about the business.
And your Orator further shew unto your Honours, that they heard
that some time afterwards, that is to say in or about the time the
Court sat at Ninety six, in April, one thousand seven hundred and
eighty five, that the said Joseph Colhoun had obtained a verdict
against the said John Lindsey, for two hundred and ten pounds,
and costs of Suit, but your Orator Robert Anderson gave himself
no trouble, concern, or uneasiness, about the said Verdict, not
feeling himself in the smallest degree individually interrested
therein, and heard nothing more of the matter, nor ever suspected
that he your Orator was considered as the said John Lindseys Bail
by any person in the world, untill about two or three weeks be
fore November Court, at Ninety Six, in the year of our Lord, one
thousand seven hundred and eighty Six, when your Orator Robert
Anderson received a Letter from John Bee Holmes Esquire, who was
concerned as Attorney for the said Joseph Colhoun, signifying that
the said Joseph Colhoun complained of not having received Satisfaction from the said John Lindsey, for the Judgement obtained as
aforesaid, and requested your Orator Robert Anderson to procure
Satisfaction for the same, as the said John Lindseys Security. And
your orator further sheweth unto your Honours, that your orator
was greatly surprized, on the receipt of the said Letter, to find
that he was considered as the said John Lindseys security, such
a thought never having entered the mind of your Orator, he could
not reconcile or believe it, untill some time afterwards, when he
your Orator conversed with the said John Bee Holmes Esquire on the
subject, when your Orator was informed, that he was certainly considered as the said John Lindseys Security; but your Orator Robert
Anderson recollecting every circumstance perfectly well, and well
knowing that he had never Signedany Bond to the Sheriff, for the
appearance of the said John Lindsey, to defend, or toabide by, or
perform, the determination of the said Suit, brought against the
said John Lindsey, and your Orator being also well convinced, that
he had never entered into, signed, nor acknowledged, any Bail
piece, or Recognisance, either before a Commissioner of Special
Bail in the Countrey, before any Judge at Chambers, or in open
Court, whereby he your Orator undertook, either by himself or
jointly, with any other person, that if the said John Lindsey was
condemned, in the action depending at Law, between the said John
Lindsey, and the said Joseph Colhoun, that he your Orator, would
render him, the said John Lindsey a prisoner in discharge of him
self, or that he your Orator, would pay it for him, and well know
ing that he had not, either in form, or substance, done, or Comm-

ited, any act, to his knowledge, or belief, that could possibly
make him responsible, to the said Joseph Colhoun as Special Bail,
or other Security, for the said John L ndsey, determined to stand
a Suit at Law. That your Orator Robert⁺Anderson not knowing or
having heard of any Affidavit, that the said Joseph Colhoun had
made, to ground an order for Bail, and not knowing, or having
heard of any order by the Court, or Judge at Chambers, to hold
the said John Lindsey to Bail; your Orator in order to be the
better satisfied, examined the Records of the said Court, to find
out whether any entry had been made, of your Orator becoming Bail
in the said Suit, when your Orator Robert Anderson found that no
such entry was made, nor any Affidavit made, by the said Joseph
Colhoun, nor oder for Bail, nor any rule or order relating thereto.
And your Orator further sheweth unto your your Honours, that soon
afterwards an Action on the case, was commenced at Law against
your orator Robert Anderson at the instance, and in the name of
the said Joseph Colhoun, wherein, the said Joseph Colhoun, by his
Declaration the said Action, set forth, That the said Joseph
Colhoun had commenced an Action, in the Court of of common pleas,
in the State aforesaid, against the said John Lindsey, and that
your Orator Robert Anderson and Thomas Brandon Esquire, had a
greed to become Special Bail, for the said John Lindsey, whereby
your orator, and the said Thomas Brandon were bound, either to
deliver the body of the said John Lindsey when called for, or to
pay such sum as might be recovered by Verdict, against him the
said John Lindsey; and that your orator Robert Anderson and the
said Thomas Brandon did become Special Bail, for the said John
Lindsey as aforesaid, by signing on the back of a copy Writ, thus
"Entered Special Bail, Robert Anderson, Thomas Brandon," And the
said Joseph Colhoun, alledging in his said Declaration, that in
fact he had recovered against the said John Lindsey, in the said
Action, wherein your Orator Robert Anderson and the said Thomas
Brandon had become Security as aforesaid, in the sum of two hundred and twenty one pounds, nine shillings, and five pence, where
upon, and by force of the undertaking of your orator Robert Anderson and the said Thomas Brandon, became liable to pay the said
sum of Two hundred and twenty one pounds, mine shillings, and five
pence, to the said Joseph Colhoun. And your orator Robert Anderson
further sheweth unto your Honours, that to the said Action your
orator plead the General Issue, Nonassumsit, and at the Court held
at Cambridge, in N vember, one thousand seven hundred and eighty
seven, the issue was tried, when the jury found a Verdict, in be
half of your said Orator and the said T omas Brandson, as Defendan
ts. And your Orator Robert Anderson, further sheweth unto your
Honours, that in November Court, one thousand seven hundred, and
eighty nine, the same cause was tried again, on a new trail granted,
when the jury found a Verdict against your said Orator, and the
said Thomas Brandon for the said sum of two hundred and twenty one
pounds, nine shillings and fivepence and costs of Suit; amounting
in the whole, to the sum of Two hundred and thirty six pounds,
eighteen shillings, and four pence, for which sum, Judgement has
been entered in the proper Office, against your said Orator, and
the said Thomas Brandon. Execution has been issued, and levied on

your said orators property; as in and by the proceeding thereon
had, in the Court of Common Pleas, aforesaid, now in the hands
of your Orator, ready to be produced to this Honourable Court,
may more fully appear and to a certified copy whereof, herewith
filed, your Orator begs leave to refer as often as occasion may
require.

But now so it is, May it please your Honours, that not with
standing the Sd. Joseph Colhoun well knows, that the Judgement
which he obtained at Law, against your orator John Lindsey, was
entirely groundless and unjust and obtained by fraud & concealment. And Altho he the said Joseph Colhoun well knows, that your
orator Robert Anderson never did, by any act, or deed, either in
form, or in substance, become Bail for the said John Lindsey; and
that your Orator Robert Anderson ought not to be in the least
responsible, or liable to discharge the same, or any part thereof.
Yet the said Joseph Colhoun, combining, and Confederating himself
with other persons to your orators unknown at present (whose names
when discovered, your orators pray may be inserted in the Bill,
with apt words, to charge each, and every of them as Defendants)
and by Connivance, Subtilty, and fraud, is endeavouring to force
your orator Robert Anderson to pay off and discharge the said
Execution, and threatens to sell the property of your Orator
Robert Anderson immediately, unless the same is paid off, and
discharged, he the said Confederate Joseph Colhoun, having had
your said orators property seized, by virtue of the said Execution
as aforesaid. (All which actings and matters, and things, of the
said Joseph Colhoun, and the other Confederates, are highly fraud
ulent, unjust, and Contrive? to Right, Equity, and good Conscience, and tend to the manifest Imposition, Injury, great opression
of your Orators. In tender consideration whereof, and for as
much as matters of this nature are more properly cognizable, and
relievable in a Court of Equity before your Honours, and in as
much as your Orators can have no relief but before your Honours,
in this Honourable Court, against the said Judgement most wrong
ful Fraudulently, and unjustly obtained, as aforesaid. And to the
end that the said Confederate, Joseph Colhoun, may true and perfect answer make, on his Corporal Oath, to all, and every the
Charges, Allegations, Chatters, and things, in this Bill charged
and contained against him, in the same manner as if the same were
hereby again repeated, and he the said Joseph Colhoun particularly
interrogated thereto, and that the said Judgement so unjustly and
unfairly and fraudently obtained, as aforesaid, against your
Orators to Vacated, and Repeated, and that in the mean time, the
property of your Orator Robert Anderson (which is threatened, and
liable to sold under Execution aforesaid) may not be disposed of;
and that all proceedings at Law against your Orator Robert Anderson touching or concerning the premises, may be staid, untill the
hearing of this cause, and further directions may be given by this
Honourable Court. And that your Orators may have all such further
and other relief in the premises, as shall be agreeable to Equity
and good Conscience. May it please your Honours, to grant unto
your Orators a Writ of Subpoena, to be directed to the said Joseph
Colhoun, and his Confederates when found out; thereby commanding

him at a certain day, and under a certain pain therein to be in
serted, personally to be, and appear, before your Honourable
Court, then and there to answer the premises, and to stand to,
and abide by, such order and Decree, therein, as to your Honours
shall seem meet. And also a Writ of Injunction, to be directed to
the said Joseph Colhoun, his Counsellers, Attorneys, Solicitors,
and Agents, and to all Sheriffs, and other Deputies, Agents,
Assistants, and Servants, thereby commanding them, and every of
them, under a certain pain, therein to be inserted, absolutely
to desist from, and stay the sale of the property levied under the
said Execution, and all proceedings at Law against your Orator
Robert Anderson, respecting the premises, till the hearing of this
cause, and further directions shall be given by your Honours.

Pendleton County   Henry Wm. Desaussure
14th April 1791   Solicitor for Complaint.

Sworn to before me
this 6th May 1791
E. ? Ramsay C.E.

This bill being alterd gamendered?in my presence is again Sworn
to this 28 April 1792.
R A Rapley C.E. S.D.

Filed May 6th, 1791.

ANSWER TO BILL OF COMPLAINT.

State of South Carolina
Upper District St.   ) In Equity

The answer of Joseph Colhoun Defendant to the amended Bill of
Complaint of Robert Anderson and John Lindsay, Complainants.

This Defendant reserving to himself now and at all times here
after all benefit of exception to the numerous errors, untruths,
and imperfections in the said amended Bill cotained for answer
Nevertheless thereunto or to so much thereof, as he is advised is
material or necessary to be answered to, answering with

That he admits that the Legislature of the State of Georgia
did pass such act as is contained in the papers A with the said
Bill filed, and at the Time and for the purposes in the said Bill
set forth, and also that the Commissioners appointed by virtue of
that Act may have given to the complainant John Lindsey such power for the collecting of confiscated property as is contained in
the paper B with the said Bill filled. But he denies that the said
John Lindsey derived from that power or from the above mentioned
act any authority to meddle with the property of John Loyd, Samuel
Loyd, Thomas Loyd Senior or Junior or of Samuel Red since none of
those persons were subjected directly to confiscation by the said

Act, as appears by the act itself, a moreperfect copy of which is marked A and herewith filed as part of this answer, and since as he is informed and firmly believes neither of those persons was ever convicted in a C_ourt of Law of the said State of Georgia, of Treasonable practices, violation of Allegiance, or assisting abetting or particularly in such practices so as to to be brought within that clause of the said act which subjects persons so convicted to do penalties.

And this Defendant further answering begs leave to observe that he conceivos the story told in the said Bill about the manner in which he became possessed of three Negroes, Jane, Jude, and Squire, therein mentioned to be of no importance to the merits or issue of this present suit, because he avers, that the action which he admits, that he did bring against the Complainant Lindsey and a copy of the proceedings in which is contained in the paper H with the Bill filed, was for the recovering of damages done to this Defendant by the said Lindsey in taking those Negroes by false & Fraudulent pretences and threats of force, out of his poss ession, where they had been lawfully placed by persons having authority so to do. In this action the proper defense, as this De- fendant is advised, was that the said Joseph Colhoun had obtained the negroes in a violent unlawfull manner from persons who had not a right to them, and that Lindsey had a right to take them either under a power from the true owners as their agent, or as confis- cated Property under his authority from the Commissioners. This is the substance of what is now alledged on that head in the Bill, and surely had this been true, it was extremely proper for all the consideration of a jury and could no doubt have been proved if true had it been necessary to examine Witnesses in Georgia, which the Complainants now pretend, this Defendant would have readily have consented to it. But no mention was made of such necessity at the Trial or before, had he refused his consent, this Court as he is advised would if applied to, have compelled him to join in such examination or the Court of Common Pleas, though not then possessed of power to order Examinations of that sort without the consent of the Parties, would on the necessary of it being made apparent to them, have continued, over the cause all such consent was obtained. The Complainants now pretend in their Bill, that affidavits which they had at the Trial of the above mentioned cause were not add- mitted in evidence. But this Defendant avers that no mention of such affidavits was made at the trial or before or as he believes hinted to the Court or his counsel. Had they been offered and been the same now produced and made Exhibits with the Complainants Bill, he is pursuaded that he should very readily have admitted them, for it was then in his power and he hopes yet is to contradict and dis- prove them by the most satisfactory Evidence even if they had been more material to the Issue of the cause, than they are Had the Loyds and Red been expressly included in the Act of Confiscation. The Act it self would have proved it, and a private copy might been given in Evidence, one indeed was in Court in possession of this Defendants Counsel who offered it to the Complainant Lindsey for

the purpose of being used as Evidence, but he thought proper to
decline it for reasons Sufficiently obvious. Had the Loyds and
Red or any of them bem convicted in the manner required by the
Act so as to bring them though not named under its penalties sure
ly the record of such conviction properly authenticated would
have been evidence to the jury, and mig have been procured in the
course of three terms, a year and a half, during which the said
suit was at Issue; no such evidence however was offered or spoken
of for the best reason possible as this defendant believes namely
because it did not exist. The complainants also pretend in their
Bill, that these negroes after being taken out of the Defendants
possession were delivered by Lindsey to the Commissioners of Confiscated Estates in Georgia. These commissioners formed a public
board whose certificates as such would have been legal Evidence
as this Defendant is advised, and he is well convinced might
easily have been produced. But the complainant Lindsey knew what
those certificates would be too well to produce them. He well
knew that the negroes had never been delivered to the commissioners, and that any certificate from them would have been Evidence
to convict instead of acquitting him, as appears from the certificates of five of them now in the Hands of this Defendants Soll-
icitor, ready to be produced and copies of which marked B & C are
herewith filed as part of this answer. Hence it fully appears as
this Defendant apprehends and begs leave to insist, that the whole
matters how alledged by the Complainants in their Bill against
the recovery of which this Defendant obtained in the above mentioned action was properly triable in that issue, proper for the
cognizance of the Jury, and fully capable of proof on the tryal
which took place had it been true. The complainants alledge in
their amended Bill and one of them, has had the rashness to swear
that this recovery was obtained by fraud, concealment and sur-
prize. They do now however point out in what the pretended fraud
consisted, and this Defendant avering as he postively does that
the verdict which he obtained against the said Lindsey was just in
his opinion and fairly obtained, and that his conduct towards the
latter was upright open and generous throughout the whole Transaction is willing to submit whether the Complainants were admitting all the have said to be true, have disclosed any circumstance
from which fraud surprise or concealment on the part of the defen
dant can possibly be inferred. They say indeed in their amended
Bill, that he received the negroe Peter, in satisfaction of the
Damages which he had sustained from Lindsey and gave no credit
for it at the Trial. This however he postively denies Peter was
delivered voluntarily at this defendants House by Red or by his
Brother in Law for him and with his consent, in compliance with
his agreement which will be hereafter particularly adverted to,
and in payment of a ballance remaining due from him to this defendant, after the previous delivery of several other negroes
the same above mentioned and taken from this Defendant by the
Complainant Lindsey. He was delivered before the cause come on,
as Lindsey well (word not plain,P.Y.) and had he been received in
satisfaction of the Damages which Lindsey had done to this Defend

ant by taking away the other negroes, certainly this might have
been proved at the Trial and would have been a good and proper
defence as far as it went. This Defence however was not set up,or
even sopken of, as the Defendant believes, and he supposes it to
be one of those after thoughts of the Complainants by which they
are now ehdeavouring to deprive him of a just, fair and Legal
verdict. As therefore this whole matter was alledged by the Complainants against that verdict, was as this Defendant is advised
properly Triable, cognizable, and capable of proof, at Law in the
action, where the verdict was obtained, he thinks it not material
to be contradicted or capable of being of being (written twice,P.Y.
inquired into here, it being as he has ever understood and begs
leave to insist a most sacred and fundamental principle of this
Courts Jurisdiction, not to interfere in cases where the parties
have a plain and adequate remedy at Law of & which they have neglected to take advantage. To do away however the violent, and un
just imputations of oppressive conduct on his part, with which
the Complainants allegations on this subject abound, he begs leave
to trouble this Honourable Court, with a relation of the manner in
which he obtained and afterwards lost the negroes in question, a
relation which he avers to be true and every part of which he make
s no doubt of being able to prove by satisfactory evidence. He will
then leave it to your Honours to Judge, how wisely the statement
made by the complainants swerves from the Truth and how consist-
ant his own conduct on the occasion has been not only with Justice and propriety, but also with lenity and disposition to foregoe
many of those advantages which the respective situation of the
parties then put into his power.

About the thirty first day of January in the year of our Lord
one thousand seven hundred and Eighty one, a party of Robbers from
the State of Georgia, belonging to that description of Men who
were then called Tories and among whom as this Defendant has
heard & believes were one Doctor Lowry and a person of the name
of Cooper, came to the Plantation of this Defendant in his absen-
ce and took away several valuable slaves some Horses and a large
quantity of wearing apparel and other effects to a considerable
amount, all of which he understood and believes, They carried into
the State of Georgia. This property belongs in part to the Defend
ant and in part to his mother and Sisters. Sometime after it was
taken away, as the Defendant is informed and believes, the negroes
consisting of two men a very likely lad named Cato, a woman and a
child, made their Escape from the Robbers, brought of the Horses
and the other effects which were plundered and were returning to
their owner this Defendant. Doctor Lowry and others of the Plundering party persued them about Little River in Georgia they fell
in with one Samuel Red Thomas Loyd and John Loyd, and perhaps some
others who under the pretence of hiding them from the pursuers and
assisting them in their return home kept them concealed near the
above mentioned place about two days and then conducted them to
the Banks of Savannah River, which it was necessary to pass over
in their return. There they took the two negroe men, whom it app-

ears they thought it would be difficult to keep on account of their attachment to their Owners, their activity and knowledge of the country and put them in a canoe with the woman and child.It was dark and the river much raised by the Rains so that the negro es in the canoe found much difficulty in gaining the opposite Bank which however they at length affected and returned to this Defendant. The boy Cato, the Horses, two valuable studs with all the other articles of cloathing, furniture &c. Red and the two Loyds with their companions carried off nor has the Defendant, or his Mother or Sisters ever regained any part of that property except one of the Horses which was restored in considerable time afterwards very much abused and injured.

The Defendant having learned into whose hands his property had fallen, found out the place of the Reds above in Georgia some distance below Augusta, and went in quest of him to obtain restitution of what he had been concerned in taking away, three other men were of the Party armed as well as this Defendant but not with intent to commit any act of violence against Red or others as is untruly stated in the Bill but for their own defence arms then being thought necessary for all persons who travelled in Georgia in order to protect them against the disultory parties of Robbers who under the name of Tories infested the country. They found Red at Home, at a house at least, which in his affidavit the paper No. 1 with the Bill filed he called his own, and which the person who now calls herself Mrs. Cattledge in her affidavit, the paper No. 2 with the Bill filed was also called Reds House, although the Bill states it to be her house and Red only to have been a Lodger with her. The Defendant then Demanded that his property or the value of it should be restored but Red at first evaded the demand and finally refused to comply with it, whereupon this Defendant in sisted on his going to the House of Colonel Elijah Clarke above Little River in Georgia, not that he might be frightened into compliance by Colonel Clarkes rigor and severity, which this Defendant never understood and does not believe to have made any part of that Officers character, nor that martial Law might be inforced against him but that he might be brought into the Neighborhood where the facts charged against him were committed and where Witnesses might be found to support or repute them. Colonel Clarke was indeed at that time, a s this Defendant well knew, absent on an Expedition against the Cherokee Indians, and it was to his House, as a proper situation, not to him in person, that Red was to go. Several offers of Settling the difference between this Defendant and the said Red by Reference disinterested and indifferent persons were made to him on the way and he was treated both on the road and at his own house with all the mildness possible, for this Defendant and his Companions had resolved to act in the most peaceable manner and to make as little appearance of Hostile intentions as armed men could possibly shew. These offers of amicable accomodation well however rejected nor does this Defendant recollect or believe that any such proposals of giving security to answer his demand as are set forth in the Bill were made on the part of of Red, or that Colonel McCoys name was mentioned, on the occasion. He, this defendant believes, but cannot certainly recollect, that some offer might have been made by Red to go before Joshua Inman as a Judge of the dispute, which however if made was certainly rejected, because Inman resided still farther than Red from where the fact was comitted and the witnesses were to be found, and also, which would have been of itself a verry sufficient reason because this Defendant knew Inman to be a person of very bad character with whom so far from referring an important Settlement to his deision he did not think it becoming to have any concern, an opinion in the event very fully justified by the fate of Inman, who has since been brought to condign and infamous punishment for his crimes. The first of these objections would also have applied and with greater force to Colonel McCoy who resided still farther than Inman, from where the facts charged against Red were committed, and if proposed as an arbitrator which this Defendant does not recollect, though it might have happened was on that account certainly and very properly rejected, when this Defendant arrived at the House of Red, he found there the three negroes Jane, Jude, and Squire in the Bill mentioned. Two of them he was informed and believes were the property of Samuel Loyd and Thomas Loyd. The Latter of whom Thomas with his Brother John had been jointly concerned with Red in taking away the Defendants property. John Loyd was at that time dead, Samuel was present at Reds, and Thomas had either fled from the United States or was in places unknown to this Defendant, who thought it just and reasonable to make the property of the Loyds answerable for the Damages which he had sustained from them. He therefore took into his Possession, the two Negroes Jane and Squire which were theirs together with the other, the woman Jude which he under stood to be Reds, in order that as some of the Loyds were already absent, and Red and Samuel Loyd might very easily abscond the whole three negroes might stand pledged for the payment of what ever damages he could fairly prove himself to have sustained. He at the same time informed Red and Samuel Loyd why this step was to be taken and told them that if the charges against them were not substantiated by indifferent Witnesses, and to the satisfaction of Judges, whom they themselves should acknowledge to be impartial, all claims against them, should be given up and their property restored. Thus it was that those Negroes came first into the possession of the Defendant.

He and his Companions with Samuel Red and the three Negroes then proceeded to Colonel Clarkes and arrived about the Eighteenth or nineteenth of September in the year one thousand seven hundred and Eighty two, immediately or verry soon after their arrival, the three men who accompanied this Defendant went Home. He and Red remained, together with the Negroes, till the saturday following, the twenty first of the same Month. Red being during this interval perfectly at Liberty, and General Clarke not at home. This Defendant had summoned a meeting of Justices and field Officers at Colonel Clarkes on the last mentioned day for deciding the dispute

between Red and him, and had also requested his Witnesses to atte
nd, having been previously advised Red to procure the attendance
of such as he might on his part have occasion for, this was the
usual and indeed the only practicable mode of deciding dusputes
about property in Georgia at that time - where the Courts of Justice had long been suspended by the violence of the war, and had
not yet resumed their functions, several field officers Justices
and others came at the day appointed and the witnesses also atten
ded. Several offers of accomodations were made by this defendant
to Red, who would not accede to any of them. This Defendant particularly offered to restore his property, and give him a general
release provided he would tell him all he knew, about the above
mentioned Robbery, and the persons concerned in it, but he refused
to do this, declaring that he would sooner satisfy the well de
mand than make any discoveries. He inquired of the witnesses atte
nding, what they knew about the facts alledged against him and
consulted with some of his friends, who were present being at
length as it appeared, convinced that the claim would be fully
substanteated against him he came to this Defendant and voluntarily offered to give him four negroes in payment for the loss of
his property and the injury done to it, the three above mentioned
immediately and the other to be delivered, some time after he said
that he would act for the Loyds to whom part of the negroes be
longed and who being jointly concerned in the plundering, ought
also to bear part in making restitution and that he conceived him
self sufficiently authorised to make a Bargain on their behalf.
This Defendant acceded to this proposition though he does not
think that the property to be given, the four negroes, was by any
means adequate to the injury which he had sustained Red entered
into a Bond for the delivery of the four negroes, three, Jane,
Jude, and Squire in the Bill mentioned were delivered immediately
and a receipt for them endorsed on the Bond, some time afterwards
Red sent the fourth to the Defendant with a Bill of Sale and he
then indorsed a receipt in full on the back of the Bond as by the
Bill of sale itself with the Bond and its several Indorsements,
all now in the hands of your Defendants Solicitor ready to be produced and, copies whereof marked D and E are herewith filed and
refered to as part of his answer will more fully appear. Before the
Bargain was concluded Samuel Loyd came of his own accord to Colone
l Clarkes and finding what Red had agreed to, gave, his consent as
far as he was concerned in the property, and declared that he ..
would undertake to act for his brother Thomas who was absent. He
added that he knew where the boy Cato was, in the creek Nation,
and would procure him and give him up to this Defendant, provided
the latter would in that case restore the two negroes, Jane and
Squire which were the property of the Loyds. To this the said Defendant agreed and the negroes were delivered by the joint consent
of Loyd & Red, whom he solemnly avers to have been through out the
whole transaction after their arrival at Clarkes free from constraint, violence, threats, or ill usuage of any kind. He carried
the negroes home & the boy Cato not being restored, retained them
till they were taken out of his possession by the Complainant

Lindsey in the manner herein after mentioned.

By these steps did this Defendant obtain possession of those negroes Steps which appear to him justifyable on every principle of property and fair dealing, and with which Red himself by his subsquent delivery of the fourth Negroe in circumstances which preclude all pretence of constraint appears to have been well content. And this Defendant is advised and begs leave to insist, that his right to those Negroes under the above mentioned delivery was sufficient in Law to authorise his retaining them against any claim of Red or the Loyds. Red and Samuel Loyd were, as he apprehends barred, from any such claim by their voluntary delivery and transfer, and had Thomas Loyd or the representatives of John brought suit for their part, he could by the Law of this State have pleaded the damages which they 'had done him in discount, and have had the amount of them deducted, out of the value of the negroes. A Deduction after which he apprehends that very little would have been left. That Red had a right to dispose of one of these negroes and he claimed no more, this Defednant firmly believes and thinks may easily be proved. He claimed and possessed that one in right of a Daughter of Thomas Loyd the elder a person who has some thought proper to call herself, and is called by the Complainants in their Bill Mrs. Oatledge, though she then lived and yet lives with Red as his wife, and was publickly acknowledged by him as such, after which this Defendant apprehends, that she will not be allowed to come into a Court of Justice and say that She was not married to him, and to reclaim property which in these circumstances he had fairly sold for in a valuable consideration.

And this Defendant further answering admits that Thomas Loyd the Elder may have made such Will as is contained in the paper E with the said Bill filed, and may have died at the time in the said Bill mentioned, leaving the said Will in full force and un altered, and that the above mentioned part of his Estate, though he does not know or believe that they were an undivided part , having always understood that one of them belonged to Red in right of his wife Elizabeth, one of the Daughters and devisees of Thomas Loyd the Elder, and that the other two belonged to Samuel and Thomas Loyd two of the sons and divisees mentioned in the said Will. From these circumstances he supposes that a division of the Testators Estate must have previously taken place, and those negroes respectively have been allotted to the last mentioned persons. And he postively denies that when the Complainant John Lindsey Demanded those Negroes from him, which he admits to have been done about the time in the Bill mentioned though by no means in a polite or civil manner, any power of attorney, or other authority from the Loyds or any of them, or from any female, or minor Heirs or devisee s of Thomas Loyd the Elder, was produced or spoken of, by the said complainant, or that he ever made mention of such persons on the contrary he founded his demand entirely on the Act of Confiscation alledged his authority from the Commissioners appointed by that

act, and affirmed that those Negroes were confiscated as part of
the Estate of Thomas Loyd Junior & John Loyd. When this Defendant
called for the act, as the most certain method of deciding whether
the property was confiscated or not, the said Lindsey refused or
evaded producing it, and observed that his word on the Subject,
as that of Gentleman might be taken. On being told how those negroes were obtained by this Defendant, and for what purposes he
held them, the said complainant Lindsey, who was then armed, as
well as two other men by whom he was accompanied, declared that he
would take them, unless prevented, by force, that it was his duty
to do so, and that he would deliver them to the Commissioners of
confiscated Estates for Wilkes and Richmond Counties, who he
doubted not, would on application, from this Defendant, do full
justice to his claim against the Loyds, a claim which at that time
the said complainant, acknowledged to be just. This Defendant at
first had thoughts of opposing their removal by force, but on more
mature consideration & advising with some of his friends he though,
t it best to desist & He however postively dehies that John Eqing
Colhoun advised the delivery of the negroes to Lindsey. That Gent
leman was indeed consulted on the subject, not as a Lawyer but as
a friend and relation of this Defendant, and a person who having
been in public life had some knowledge of confiscation Laws, and
his Answer was, that if these Negroes were under confiscation
Lindsey had a right to take them, otherwise not, but he could give
no opinion about their being in that predicament, because Lindsey
could not or would not produce the act, though he was requested
to do so more than once or twice. I$_n$deed if Mr. Colhouns sentiments or advise concerning this transaction could be of any weight
in deciding this cause it might easily be inferred from his subsquent conduct, for when acting for the State as the Attorney
Generals Deputy in Ninety Six Court, he preferred an Indictment for
a cheat against the said Lindsey which Indictment was found by the
grand Jury, on account of this very Business of taking the Negroes,
and will hereafter be more particularly adverted to and when that
prosecution was dropt in the manner and for the reasons stated be
low, he made an affidavit whereon to found an order for bail in a
civil action for the same cause, as appear more fully below, and
in the papers hereinafter taken notice of, and this Defendant can
not avoid remarking here the extreme inconsiderateness with which
the complainants seem to have framed their allegations in this and
other instances, nor from expressing his surprise that they would
be very unadvised as to bring forward Mr. Colhoun to vouch for
them in a transaction which he has made the foundation of a crime
inal prosecution, and this Defendant further answering admits that
the said Lindsey, took away the negroes in question, but postively
denies that he the Defendant ever consented or meant to consent
to their removal, or in any manner authorised it. He also postive
ly denies that he took any receipt from Lindsey for those negroes
in any manner whatever. Lindsey indeed as this Defendant after
wards found, wràte a receipt as nearly as he can recollect in the
following words " recev'd from Joseph Colhoun three negroes Jane,
Jude, and Squire the property of the Loyds." This he signed but

not as agent for the commissioners on the Loyds and Left it on
the Defdendants table who never received, or intendedto receive
it, nor was it written or left with his consent. Through the whole
of this Eransaction, the said Lindsey made no mention of his acting in behalf of Thomas Loyd Seniors Orphans or Legatees; and this
Defendant begs leave here to bring into view of this honourable
Court another instance of the great rashness and inconsistance
with which the complainants have framed their Bill. They alledge
that one of them, Lindsey, took possession of these negroes in
the double capacity of agent for the commissioners, and for the
Legatees of Thomas Loyd Seniors, whereas it is evident that un
less they were confiscated, the commissioners would have no right
to them and that if they were, then Thomas Loyds representatives
could have none. In another part of their Bill, they afirm that
Red was only a Lodger at the house of Mrs. Catledge and then file
two affidavits the papers No. 1 and 2 in which these persons both
swear that the house was Reds. So they file an affidavit of the
Complainant Lindsey, paper No. 5 in which he swears that Samuel
Loyd left this Country and never returned, and then in one of the
amendments to their Bill they State on oath that Samuel Loyd did
return and come to this Defendants.

And this Defendant further answering, postively denies that the
boy Peter was received in consequence of any arbitration, between
him and Red, whom he never saw since the above mentioned Bond was
signed and between whom and him no overtures, conversation or
correspondence about any arbitration passed subsequent to that
period. That boy was delivered at the Defendants house by a person
whom Red sent for that purpose out of Georgia, and delivered in
payment of the fourth negroe due to the Defendant under the Condition of the above mentioned Bond, nor did he ever conceive such
an idea as that the boy was to go in-discharge of the whole or any
part of the damages done to him by L,ndsey, or hear such a proposition which if he had heard he certainly would have rejected. He
admits that the said John Lindsey may possibly have been informed
and have believed the three Negroes in question to have been ·
confiscated as part of the Estate of Thomas Loyd Senior and may
have possibly have taken them away, as the Bill states, without
any evil design and with intent to restore them to the commission
ers of confiscated Estates. But he thinks it extremely improbable,
almost incredible indeed, that such a belief could have existed
in the mind of a man who pretended as Lindsey did, when he took
the negroes away, to have about him the act of confiscation where
no such names as those of Loyd or Red appear, and who acted as he
now pretends, under the authority and by the advice of commission
ers some of whom at Least, as appears by their certificates the
exhibits B and C above filed and now referred to never supposed
that property to be under Confiscation. As to Lindsey's intentions
about the disposal of those negroes, this Defendant does not certainly know what they may have been, having no other method of
guessing at them but from his conduct, which seems very fully to
demonstarte a very different motive, from that assigned in the

Bill states merely from a sense of duty, without any sole designs
any wish to injure this Defendant or benefit himself but took the
negroes with intent to deliver them up to the Commissioners, which
this Defendant does not know or believe to have been the case, it
is in his opinion very difficult to conceive why such delivery
was not made. That it never took place appears from the certificat
es of five commissioners, the exhibits B and C above filed and
refered to the Bill indeed states that when the Negroes were
carried over from this Defendants into Georgia, no baord of Commissioners were sitting, and that till one could be convened, it
was thought best to leave them with their former owners. But sure
ly it would have been much more safe and proper to place them with
some of the commissioners who resided in Wilkes or Richmond Counties nearer than Mrs. Catledges to where they had been brought
from, than to carry them to her forty or fifty miles below Augusta,
and it seems very extraordinary to this Defendant that negroes
seized as confiscated property should be placed for safe keeping
with the very persons from whom they were taken, or that the Complainants could have considered Red and the Loyds, persons whom in
their Bill they declare to be great villains, known and declared
enemies, as proper depositories of public property. But say the
complainants security was taken, this Defendant however begs leave
to ask how it is possible to suppose that such persons as Red and
the Loyds, are represented by the complainants to have been, whose
whole propertythey declare to have been under Confiscation, could
find good security for the delivery of that property, from these
circumstances and many others, this Defendant is of opinion and
thinks it may be satisfactorily proved that Lindsey so far from
taking those Negroes with intent to deliver them to the Commission
ers came for the express purpose and by previous agreement to get
them from this Defendant under pretence of their being Confiscated
a pretence which in this Defendants opinion he knew to be false
and then delivered them to the Loyds or Red or some other person
for them and he is informed and believes, and hopes to prove that
they were actually delivered or some of them to Joshua Inman the
person mentioned in the Bill who as this Defendant believes appears
throught to have been a confederate with Lindsey in the Business.

And this Defendant further answering sayeth that he does not
know or believe that the said Complainant Lindseys conduct in pla-
cing the negroes with the person whom he calls Mrs. Catledge was
approved by any of the Commissioners of Confiscated Estates in
Georgia except the said Thomas Lewis who never actes as a commissioner though appointed and who this Defendant admits may have received such letter from Lindsey on the subject and returned such
answer as are set forth in the Bill. The circumstances however and
time when the Letters were written carry, in this Defendants opini
on, strong marks of fraud. Why are the Letters, one of these at
least, without date? Why is not the second letter written by Lindsey to Lewis produced as well as the first? for by Lewis's letter
he appears to have received two. Why was not this Letter of Lewis's
or of Lindseys to him produced at the Trial between the latter and

and this Defendant? How did Lindsey, not usually, very exact in
his Business happen to retain a copy of his first letter to Lewis
and not of the other? Why did not Lewis give an answer to the
first letter till a second was written, for the purpose as it appears, of obtaining an answer? These questions as this Defendant
apprehends, cannot be answered but by recurring to a supposition
which he believes to be well founded that the whole of this correspondence is a fabrication subsequently contrived between Lindsey
and Lewis for the purpose of giving some Colour of Plausibility to
the present application. As to Samuel Red, this Defendant postive
ly denies that he never pretended any right to any of the negroes
in question. On the contrary he always affirmed to this Defendant
that one of them named Jude, was his property in right of his Wife,
the person whom the complainants in their Bill now call Mrs. Catledge tho when the negroes were received from Red, she lived with
him as his wife and was so reputed, and acknowledged, by him.
Whether Red was a party in taking away this Defendants property
he does not certainly know, but he believes it to have been the
case, and believes it as he apprehends, or very sufficient grounds
That he did bring such action against the complainants John Lindsey
as is set forth and contained in the paper H with the Bill filed.
He admits also that he obtained a verdict therein and soon after
wards entered up his Judgement. But he postively denies that there
was any fraud, connivance or concealment used on his part in obtaining the said verdict, or that any evidence offered by Lindsey
in support of his defense was prevented from going to the Jury.
The evidence indeed now talked of, namely the affidavits and letters filed with the Bill, were not then produced or mentioned. The
Act of Confiscation was indeed called for by the court. But Lindsey did not think proper to produce it, though it was offered to
him by Major Pinckney, this Defendants then counsel. The Complainants say they are unable to conceive on what legal or just grounds
the said verdict was given or how the jury could be induced to
find it. This Defendant supposes that very legal and just grounds
may be found, in this answer and in the evidence given, and that
the jury acted under the influence of the same conviction which
had been before induced a Grand Jury, as will hereafter appear,
find an indictment for a cheat against Lindsey on account of this
very transaction. The Bill States that this Defendant pretended
this thing and pretended that, to the Jury in order to obtain the
said verdict. But surely neither this Honourable Court, or the
complainants need be told that Juries do not find verdicts on the
pretenses of the Plaintiff without proof. The verdict, this Defend
ant apprehends must be taken as full evidence that sufficient
proof was given, and he avers that every material charge on which
the said action was founded, was supported by respectable witness
es. He did not charge Lindsey with having claimed the negroes as
his own or derived any pecuniary advantage from the disposal of
them, nor does he know, though he very strongly suspects that to
have been the case. The action which he brought was for taking the
negroes out of his possession under colour of false and fraudulent
representatives, which he avers to have been fully proved and he

postively denies that he freely and voluntarily delivered them to
Lindsey, who took them without his permission or consent, and declared that he would do so unless prevented by force of arms, that
Lindsey never returned those negroes to the commissioners of confis
cated Estates, nor intended to do so. This Defendant verily believ
es for the reasons stated above and from the best information which
he has been able to obtain.

And this Defendant further answering admits that the above ment
ioned action was referred to arbitration in the manner and at the
time mentioned in the Bill and afterwards returned into court be
cause the Arbitrators for some reasons which he does not now recollect did not make an award. He also admits that the complainant
Lindsey the then Defendant may possibly have been ignorant of the
mode at that time of obtaining the testimony of Witnesses Residing
out of this state, but he thinks it very improbable that such ignor
ance should exist considering the skill and ability of the said
Lindseys then counsel, and he submits whether the voluntarily igno-
rance of the said Lindsey about the Law, can alter the justice of
the case, or authorize the interferance of this Court. One thing he
postively avers that Lindsey neither at the trial or before made
the least mention of any affidavits that he wished to produce of
any witnesses in Georgia that he wished to examine, or of any testimony that he wished to obtain from thence, and this Defendant be
lieves that the said Lindsey was too conscious of the atrocity of
his own conduct, to wish at that time or now, for it is to further
inquired into than it was, or any more evidences to be produced
than actually went to the jury. The complainants may be of opinion
for any thing that this Defendant knows, that he had no foundation
in Law or justice for an action against Lindsey, and that the jury
had the whole truth of the case gone before them, could not have
found the verdict that was given. If however this be the opinion
of Colonel Anderson, he must lately have altered his sentiments
very much upon the subject, as appears by an affidavit marked F.
and herewith filed and referred to, where he is proved to have
declared that this Defendant had been ill used by Lindsey. As to
an order for Bail in the said suit this Defendant admits that none
was made, not however for want of an affidavit, for one was made,
and a very sufficient one as this Defendant is advised, and it
appears in one of the complainants own exhibits the paper I with
the Bill filed. And he begs leave to state to this Honourable Court
the reasons why no order for bail was taken though intended to be
given. The first proceeding commenced against the said John Lindsey
at the instance of this Defendant, for taking away the negroes in
question, was an Indictment for a cheat, which was found by the
Grand Jury, and traversed by the said Lindsey, the then Defendant
as appears by the record of it marked G and herewith filed & referred to. Afterwards this Defendant was induced to drop this criminal prosecution, and commence a civil suit for damages, but he
consented to this at the request of Lindsey and his friends, and
upon the express Condition that Special Bail should be given, by
which this Defendant postively avers that he did not mean security,

for Lindseys appearance at the next Court, as the Bill sets forth,
but Bail to abide the event of the suit, such Bail as is more
particularly termed in Law, as this Defendant is advised, Bail
above or Bail to the Action. Such Bail was agreed by Lindsey to be
given, such Bail this Defendant instructed his counsel Mahor
Pinckney to take. That gentleman always informed him, and he al
ways understood that it was taken, hor would he on any terms have
dropt the criminal prosecution. In what Situation, with what in
tent, or under what belief and opinion the complainant Colonel
Anderson signed the memorandum special Bail, this Defendant does
not know, for he neither was present at the transitory, or knew
any thin of it, till it was over. He did not know that Colo. Anderson was to be or had been applied to on the subject, till he
heard it from his counsel, after the Business was settled and the
memorandum signed. All that this Defendant knows on the subject
is that Major Pinckney always told him that Colonel Anderson and
Colonel Brandon were Lindseys Special Bail, that Lindsey frequent
ly declared the same thing, and that Colo. Brandon often acknowledged it, nor did this Defendant ever know that there was any
informality in the Business till long after and he submits whether
it can be supposed that the said complainant Anderson under the
circumstances of the case and the parties, could have viewed this
engagement in the light of a Security for Lindseys personal appear
ance. The said complainant is well known to be a man much conver-
sant with business and by no means ignorant of Law. The common,
though not, legal acceptation of the term special Bail is Bail to
the action, in this acceptation the said complainant as this Defendant conceives must often have heard, and well understood it, and
he must also have well known, as this Defendant supposes that mere
Bail to appear in a suit Bail to the Sheriff is never taken on a
sheet of paper but by a Bond to the Sheriff. From these circumstances this Defendant verily believes that the Bill, must have known
perfectly well what he was about when he was about when he signed
the above mentioned memorandum. But if he did not, if he was so
incautious as to sign a paper, the legal effects of which he did
not understand, surely it was his own fault, and the Loss ought to
fall on him, not on this Defendant, who if any fraud connivance or
circumvention was practised in obtaining the said memorandum to be
signed, which he does not know or believe to have been the case,
was wholly ignorant of and unconcerned in it. He is indeed at a Loss
to conjecture on whom the complainant means to throw the imputations of those frauds and acts of circumvention by which he preten
ds to have been assailed, surely it cannot be on the Defendant who
according to the complainants own allegations was not present or
concerned in procuring the said memorandum surely it cannot be
Major Pinckney who was them this Defendants attorney and transacted
the business and whom the complainant will scarcely be hardy enough
as this Defendant supposes, to charge with fraud. It must then be
Lindsey himself who committed the fraud, if any were committed,
who deceived and took in the said complainant. And this Defendant
submits whether he can or ought to be injured by the fraud of
Lindsey, or whether any fact is disclosed in the Bill from which
fraud even on the part of the Latter can in this instance be
inferred.

And this Defendant further answering admits that when the Judgement
had been for some time entered up against the said Lindsey and
no payment made, two several Writs one of Fieri Facias and the
other, the second of Capias ad Satisfacilndum were issued against
him at the instance of this Defendant and duly lodged in the
Sheriffs Office, who made on them the respective returns of Nulla
bond and Non Est Inventus. This Defendant thereupon ordered his
Attorney Mr. Holmes to have recourse to the Bail, and learned for
the first time, that on account of some informality in taking it
the persons whom he considered as Bail could not be made answerable
as such, but by signing the memorandum special Bail with intent to
become Bail to the action had rendered themselves liable to pay
the Judgment of the Defendant did not pay it or surrender himself
in Execution. What the effect of such signing may be in Law this
Defendant professes himself unable to determine. The Court of
Common Pleas and a jury of the country, he always understood and
now believes to be the proper and only tribunal for deciding such
a point, which he is advised and apprehends to be a mere question
of Law and fact. The question of fact being whether the parties
signed that memorandum under circumstances, and in a manner from
which an intent to become securities, and the question of Law,
whether the signing under such circumstances would render them
liable to an action for the amount of the Judgment if the Debtor
did not pay it, or render himself himself in execution. In order
to obtain from this tribunal a decision on those points and to in
force the contract if it should be established and adjudged binding
in Law, this Defendant admits that he commenced such action against
the said Robert Anderson, and against Colonel Brandon the other
person who signed the memorandum as is mentioned in the Bill and
set forth in the paper K therewith filed, but he positively denies
that he knew or believed the Judgment which he had obtained again
st John Lindsey the complainant to be unfair or void of foundation
in Justice, or that the said Robert Anderson the other complainant
had not intentionally and voluntarily done any act by which in
form or substance he became liable to answer in nature of Bail to
the action for Lindsey or that the said last mentioned complainant
never considered himself, as so liable, ought not in justice to be
made so, or never entertained the most distant idea, as he says of
ever being called on as such. On the contrary this Defendant firm
ly believes that when the said complainant Anderson signed the
memorandum in question he did intend to become Bail to the action
for Lindsey and knew perfectly well the nature of that Contract and
what he was doing when he entered into it, and he is also of opinion, that the said Anderson, was and is liable in justice as well
as Law to stand in the situation of such Bail because by his signing in the manner above mentioned, this Defendant was prevented
from exacting other Bail from the said Lindsey which in all proba-
bility would have been procured. Of this opinion were the Court
and Jury which tried the issue in the last mentioned action between
the said complainant and this Defendant for the nature and objects
of which he refers to the paper K and other documents with the Bill
filed, appear evidently to have been, for no doubt as this Defend

ent understood and believes was entertained about the signing or
the intent with which it was made. They were fully proved and be
lieved to have seensuch as this Defendant stated. But the Judge
who then presided, directed the jury that admitting the signing
and intent, which were both proved, yet on account of some fatal
informallity they could not in Law constitute such a contract as
would supply the place of Bail to the action and render the parties
liable as such, and that therefore a verdict must be found for the
Defendants which this Defendant admits was done, not on any doubt
which the jury entertained about the facts, but from the Direction
of the Judge on the question of law. This opinion of the Judge was
consideredas erronious and a misdirection, and on that ground a
new trial was moved for by this Defendants councel, before all the
Judges then in the State as he is informed, who unanimously revers
sed the former deciscion, declared that the memorandum in question
signed in the circumstances that attended it though not regularly
Bail, which this Defendant did not charge it to be, did constitute
in Law a firm and binding contract on the signers, to become answe
rable for Lindsey, in the nature of Bail to the action, that is, to
pay the Judgment if he did not pay it or render himself in executio
n, that the Plantiff this Defendant had a good ground of action and
a right to recover, and finally ordered a new trial, which this
Defendant admits was had at the time mentioned in the Bill, and in
which a verdict was given in his favour under the direction of
Mr. Justice Grimkie who then presided, for the amount of the Judgment against Lindsey with Interest on it and costs of suit. This
Defendant on this verdict admits that he afterwards caused Judgment
to be entered up, and the said Robert Anderson and Thomas Brandon
neglecting to make any payment, caused an Execution to be issued
against their goods for the satisfaction of the said Judgment, as
he thought and still thinks himself well justiable in doing. And
he begs leave to submit, whether the whole subject matter of this
last suit, as well as of his said action against Lindsey, was not
even according to the shew.ing of the complainants themselves,
properly and fully Triable at Law, capable of proof before the respective juries and proper for the decision of the court of Common
Pleas, even fraud had any existed in the several transactions, on
which these suits were founded, is as he is advised, and begs leave
to submit, fully cognizable in the Court of Law, where it may and
will be relieved against on any circumstances being proved on which
it can fairly be inferred. And he further submits whether any such
circumstances are disclosed in the Bill or can be presumed to exist,
even from the statement of the complainants themselves and whether
this court step so far beyond the bounds of its jurisdiction as to
take Cognizance of matters not only properly triable but already
fully gried, heard and determined by a court of competant jurisdiction and powers to have given all the relief to which the parties
have even alledged a right. As to the general charges of fraud so
roundly and as this Defendant thinks so unguardedly made in the
Bill, he is advised and begs leave to submit, that they can be of
no avail since were such general charges admitted to give this

court jurisdiction, without a disclosure of circumstances from which it might appear what the fraud was, or whether it existed, there could not possibly be a case descided at Law which might not afterwards by vague and general charges of fraud be drawn into this Court.

And as to the said John Lindsey's part in the present application this Defendant, begs leave to state that after the last mentioned Judgment was obtained against his Bail as securities Messrs. Anderson and Brandon, he was so well satisfied with the justice of this Defendants recovery against himself, that he wrote to this Defendant from Georgia and made a promise of payment as appears by his Letter on the subject, now in the hands of this Defendants Solicitor ready to be produced and a copy of which marked H is herewith filed and referred to as part of this answer. This Letter the Defendant begs leave to insist ought to be considered in this court as full release and relinquishment on the part of the said Lindsey of all right to relief against the said recovery of such a right ever had existance and this Defendant hopes, there fore that the Bill as far as it relates to Lindsey, will be dismissed with costs. He indeed has good reasons to believe and is of opinion that Lindsey in fact has no part in this application, that his name was used by the other complainant without authority, and that the Bill was drawn and filed without his knowledge. This defendant indeed hopes that this may be the case, for the said Bill puts a number of assertions into the mouth of Lindsey, so utterly and notoriously false, that he is willing to suppose the latter in capable of having altered them him self or authorized their witne sses. And he prays to be hence dismissed with his reasonable costs an charges by him in this behalf most wrongfully sustain.

The said Defendant Joseph Colhoun being duly sworn before me on his oath, said that the facts, matters & allegations in the above answer contained and set forth are true. as far as relates to his own act and deed, that he believes them to be true as far as relates to the act and deed of other persons.
Joseph Colhoun

Robert Goodloe Harper
Solicitor for the Defendant

Sworn to before me this
30 April 1793
R A Rapley C.E. (L.L.)

CLERK OF COURTS OFFICE, ABBEVILLE, S.C.

Georgia
Burke County) By virtue of a Commission issuing from the Honorable
the Court of Equity for the District of Ninety six in the State of
South Carolina to Edward Weathers, Isaac Perry, Henry Hughes, John
Bowden and Daniel Evans directed for the examination of Witnesses
in a cause there depending between John Lindsay and Robert Anderson
Complainants and Joseph Colhoun Defendant. We Isaac Perry, John
Bowden and Henry Hughes the Acting Commissioners under the said
Commissioner and also the respective Clerks by us employed in transcribing and engrossing the said Depositions, having first sever-
ally taken the Oaths annexed to the said Commission according to
the true yenor & effect thereof & as thereby required.

Onthe part and behalf of the Complainants John Lindsay and
Robert Anderson, James Red of Burke County in the State of Georgia
aged forty eight years and upwards, being produced, Sworn and examined at the house of Alexander Carter of Waynesborough in the County
aforesaid Tavern keeper on the 24th October A.D. 1790 - Deposeth
and saith as follows.

1st. In answer to the first Interrogatory this Deponent saith,
That he never knew Jane and Squire untill after they were brought
back from S. Carolina, but Jude he had known for some considerable
time living with Elizabeth Cartledge. That he knows that his Brother Samuel Red has no right to the said three negroes Jane, Jude and
Squire, neither had he ever any right to the said three negroes, nor
any of them, to his, this Deponents knowledge and belief, neither
does he believe that his said Brother Samuel Red ever claimed any
right to the said three negroes nor any of them at any time, nor
ever pretended any claim or right to any part thereof. That when
the said three negroes were brought back from So. Carolina, as he
believes by the Complainant John Lindsay, Jane and Squire were
taken into the possession of Joshua Inman under the pretence of his
having bought them from Samuel Loyd, and since remained in the possession of him and his Heirs untill within a few years past, when
Patience Loyd obtained possession of Squire, who has since run from
her, but she has commenced Suit for the recovvry of Jane and her
issue and Jude still lives with Elizabeth Cartledge.

2nd. In answer to the second Interrogatory this Deponent saith,
That he always understood that the said three negroes Jane, Jude and
Squire did belong to Thomas Loyd Senr. in his lifetime and since his
death that they are part of his Estate which is yet undivided, but
his youngest Daughter Patience Loyd, now Patience Mathis, has obtained letters of administration on the said Estate and (as he
supposes) will shortly bring about a division of the said Estate
among the different Legatees, which has still yet been omitted. That
two of the Sons of the said Thomas Loyd Senior Deceased, namely John
and Thomas were considered Enemies to the Country in the late war,
this Deponent further saith that he always heard and he believes

John got his dividend of the Estate, and that the negroes Jane, Juxe,
& Squire were not in any manner the property of the said John, neither had he any part thereof - it was generally supposed the property of the said John and Thomas was liable to the Confiscation Law.

3rd. In answer to the third Interrogatory this Deponent, that
he does not know that he had ever heard of the Defendant Joseph
Colhoun untill he heard of his carrying off his said Brother Samuel
Red a prisioner from his own house, with the three negroes above
mentioned, but never saw him untill some time afterwards at Augusta.

4th. In answer to the fourth Interrogatory this Deponent saith,
that in or about the month of September 1782, the next day after
his brother Samuel Red was carried off, he heard that the Defendant
Joseph Colhoun with an Armed party had come to his Said Brothers
house the day before, had taken him a Prisioner, threatened to kill
him, and had carried him off with the said three negroes Jane, Jude
and Squire, which were then at his House in the possession of Elizabeth Cartledge, Patience Loyd and Samuel Loyd, three of the children of Thomas Loyd Senr. Decesd. but where they were carried to he
never heard, untill his said Brother Samuel came back, who told him
that he had been carried to Colo. Clarkes and detained there a
Prisioner about three weeks, expecting every day to be put to death.
And that the Defendant Colhoun had compelled him to sign some bond,
as he the said Samuel believed for the delivery of one Negroe at
some future time, but that he could not be certain what the said
Bond was for, as he could not read writing himself, was among
Strangers, all of whom were his Ehemies, and they read the Bond to
him for one negroe, but let it be for what it would, he was glad to
sign it, in hopes to save his life and obtain his Liberty, and that
he was not liberated as he expected he would be, when he signed the
Bond, but was still kept a prisioner untill he made his Escape. That
he cannot recollect what his said Brother Samuel Red told him about
the three negroes Jane, Jude and Squire, but thinks he understood
they were left at Colo. Clarkes.

5th. In answer to the fifth Interrogatory this Deponent saith,
That he had heard & understood that the Complainant John Lindsay
was Commissioner and authorised to bring back such Confiscated property as had been plundered and carried away, and also the property
of Orphans which had been plundered and carried away. And he still
understood and believed that the said John Lindsay did recover or
get the said three negroes from the Defendant Colhoun in So. Carolina and did bring them back, as Elizabeth Cartledge got Jude and
still has her, but Jane & Squire were sold to Joshua Inman by Samuel
Loyd, who pretended to claim them, and after their return were kept
by said Inman and his Heirs untill lately, when Patience Loyd atte-
mpted to obtain a division of the Estate among the Legatees.

6th. In answer to the sixth Interrogatory this Defendant saith
that he knows and is well persuaded that the Complainant John

Lindsey did not convert any of the said negroes to his own use or
benefit, neither directly or indirectly, neither can he believe or
suppose that he ever received any reward from the Commissioners of
Confiscated Estates for bringing back the said negroes, for altho
he understood they were left by the Complainant Lindsey on the
Condition that they should be delivered to the said Commissioners
when called for by them, yet as they did not demand, nor take the
said negroes into their possession as confiscated property, he the
Deponent saith he cannot suppose that they would reward any person
for bringing them back.

    7th & 8th. In answer to the seventh and eighth Interrogatories
this Deponent saith that the Defendant Joseph Colhoun did show this
deponent a Bond, which he took in his hand and read over. The said
Bond had a considerable penalty or Obligation binding on his said
Brother Samuel Red to compell the delivery of one negroe to the
Defendant Colhoun between the age of twelve and twenty years, and
their was no credit upon the said Bond and only one Negroe mentioned in the Condition thereof. That his said Brother Samuel Red
told him this Deponent that the Bond afores.d was estorted from
him by the said Defendant Colhoun through fear and Compulsion,
when he the said Saml. was a Prisoner and in great fear of his
life, which information this Deponent saith he verily believes to
be true, because about the last of May 1783 his said Bro. Samuel
applied to him this Deponent to go to Augusta to meet with the
Deft. Joseph Colhoun, to settle the matter with him if possible
and to get up his the sd. Samls. Bond, for the negroe as aforesaid
from the said Defendant Colhoun. That when his said Brother Saml.
Red made said application, he told him this Deponent that he was
afraid to meet with the Defendant Colhoun again, least he would
again make him a Prisoner- take his life, or ill treat him other
wise as he had done before, saying at the same time, that he would
give him this $^{Dept.}$ his negroe fellow Antony (a very valuable
negroe man) if he would and settle it for him, for he would give
up all he had before he the said Samuel would go himself. And
further said that Jonathan Gift had come from the Defendt. Colhoun
at Augusta, and had told him the said Samuel that if he did not
come up to Augusta immediately and discharge his Bond, he would
be down upon him again. That he this Deponent went to Augusta at
the request of his said Brother Samuel and met with the Defendant
Colhoun, General Pickens and General Twiggs being present, the
latter of which he chose as an Arbitrator & he believes the former
had been chosen by the Defendant Colhoun, but they did not attempy
to meet on the business, or to take evidence on either side concerning the said differences about to be submitted to them, but
advised them to settle their own disputes. This Deponent further
saith that he still insisted to the Defendant Colhoun that his
Brother Sam. Red (in whose behalf he met him there) had never
injured him the said Deft. Colhoun, neither in person family nor
property, therefore he the said Colhoun had no right to receive
any payment, however after much altercation, this Deponent saith
he agreed to discharge the said Bond, supposing it must be done as
it had been given by his said Brother Samuel, and the Defendant

Colhoun agreed to take one negroe from the age of twelve to twenty
years agreeable to the Condition of the said Bond, and agreed to
wait some short time, in getting good Security that such a negroe
should be punctually delivered to him at his House in Long Cane by
a certain time, perhaps in ten or fifteen days of the date. That
General Twiggs became his this Deponents Security, and that he this
Deponent did actually carry a Negroe Girl of that description him
self to the house of the Defendant Colhoun at Long Cane, within the
time to which he was bound, but the said Defendant Colhoun refused
to take or receive the said negroe Girl, altho she was country born,
likely, smart and sensible and between the ages stipulated, yet this
Deponent saith he offered five Guineas in ready cash with the
Wench rather than to bring her back and carry up another, it being
near one hundred miles distant from where he lived, but the Defendant Colhoun would not receive her upon any terms, but consented to
let him have longer time on his agreeing to send him a negroe Boy
with a Bill of Sale executed and by one of the Subscribing Witness
es to the same, That he the Defendant Colhoun might get it proved
by his Evidence, when he received it with the Negroe Boy, or which
Conditions the Deft. Colhoun did punctually promise and agree to
and with this Deponent to send his Brother San. Red's Bond for the
negroe aforesd. by the return of the person who would bring the
negroe Boy and Bill of Sale as aforsaid. And this Deponent saith
that he did send a likely valuable negroe Boy named Peter and a
Bill of Sale within the time agreed upon by Samuel Loyd one of the
Subscribing Witnesses to the said Bill of Sale agreeable to Bargain.
but the Defendant Colhoun Colhoun (written twice P.Y.) did not send
the said Bond, but wrote by Samuel Loyd to this Deponent, that he
did not mean any advantage by keeping back the Bond, but he would
be at Augusta in a few weeks and if he did not meet him this De-
pment there, he might defend he would bring or send it to his this
Deponents house. And this Deponent further saith that he has never
yet received the said Bond, nor heard from the said Defendant since,
altho he has wrote and sent to him for it by every good opportunity
but he cannot know his reasons for detaining the said Bond. That
the Defendant Joseph Colhoun appeared to be fully satisfied with
the negroe Boy Peter delivered to him by Saml. Loyd as aforesaid, at
least he never expressed any dissatisfaction to this Deponents know
ledge, after he agreed to be satisfied with the discharge of the
Bond at Augusta as aforesaid, but before that Viz at Augusta he
spoke of great hopes and spoke of the three negroes Jane, Jude and
Squire being taken out of his hands, which he the Defendant said
he held as Security for the return of all his property - but this
Deponent saith that as he verily believed and was well convinced
in his own mind that his Brother Samuel Red (in whose behalf he met
the Defendant Colhoun as afor.sd.) had never injured him the sd.
Colhoun in the smallest degree & knowing that his said Brother had
not claimed any right in the three negroes aforsaid, and knowing
or understanding that the Defendant Colhoun had forcibly carried off
the said three negroes when he first made his Brother a Prisoner at
his own house as afersd. he therefore insisted that it was cruel
to totally ruin his said Brother Samuel without any the least cause,
upon which the Defendant consented to take the one negroe as specified in the Bond as aforesaid as a full satisfaction for his losses

altho he still said that it was not equal to his whole losses.

9th. In answer to the ninth Interrogatory this Deponent saith that he did hear that the Defendant Colhoun had commenced an Action at Law in So. Carolina against the Complainant Lindsey, at which he was much surprised, as he still understood and believed that the Defendant Colhoun had just taken the said negroes into his possession by force and violence, and as he well knew that the said Colhoun had actually agreed to take one negroe which he did actually receive. But this Defendant saith that he was more surprised when he heard that the Defendant Colhoun had obtained a verdict agt. the said Complainant Lindsey for that, or some other considerable sum of money.

10th. In answer to the tenth and last Interrogatory this Deponent saith, that he verily believes that his said Brother Samuel Red never plundered nor took any of the property in his possession. Because if his said Brother Samuel had actually plundered the Defendant Colhoun, or if he had taken, or kept any of the said Colhouns property in his possession, this Deponent saith he verily thinks he must have heard something of it, by some person or persons besides the Defendant Colhoun or he must have seen the property if he had kept it at his own house = he being frequently there, but he never heard of such a thing being imputed to his said Brother, only by the Defendant Joseph Colhoun at Augusta as aforesaid. And this Deponent further saith not.

The aforegoing Deposition taken   Isaac Perry
the 24th October 1793.   John Douten
                                       Henry Hughes

On the part and behalf of the Defendant Joseph Colhoun, the said James Red being produced, sworn and examined on the Cross Interrogatories accompanying the said Commission, Deposeth and saith as follows.

1st. In answer to the first Interrogatory this Deponent saith That he does believe that the Defendant Joseph Colhoun, by imprisonment, threats, and such like usuage and extortion Bond from his said Brother Samuel Red, so his said Brother Samuel Red told him after he returned from Colo. Clarkes, where he had been carried to from his own house, and confined as a Prisoner by the Defendant Colhoun, which information he verily believes to be the truth with out any covering or prevaricating on his said Brother's part. Because about the Month of May following, when his said Brother Samuel Red came and applied to him this Deponent (in only receiving a Message) to meet the Defendant Colhoun at Augusta and to settle the matter some how in his behalf, that then his said Brother Samuelseemed so exceedingly alarmed that he the Deponent has no doubt but he would have given up all his property before he would again put himself in the power of the said Defendant Colhoun after the treatment he had formerly received from or by the means of the said Defendant Colhoun, when he was before confined as a Prisoner. But the Deponent saith that he heard that the said Defend.t Colhoun

with an armed Party carried off his said Brother Samuel a Prisioner
from his own house by force and violence, by many different people
as well as by his Brother Samuel, and he verily believes it to be
the truth, as he has not the least reason to doubt its being so.
This Deponent farther saith that he does not know of any damages
ever done by the Loyds to the Defendant Joseph Colhoun, and he is
well persuaded that his Brother Samuel Red never did him the least
damage, indeed he has not the smallest reason to think he did, there
fore the Bond must have been extorted from him & could not have been
given voluntarily in consideration of any damages.

2nd. In answer to the second Interrogatory this Deponent saith
that he does not believe that his Brother Samuel Red ever delivered
Jane, Jude and Squire, or any of them in the discharge of that or
any other Bond, becasue his said Brother Samuel never had any right
or title to them or any of them, to his this Deponents knowledge and
belief. This Deponent further saith that he never saw any Bond to
compell the payment of any thing by his said Brother Samuel Red to
the Defendant Joseph Colhoun, only the one which the said Defendt.
Colhoun produced at Augusta when he attended to settle the matter
with him, in the behalf of his said Brother Samuel Red — the Bond
then produced had no credit entered upon its Back, neither was there
any mention made of any but one negroe in its inside, but the Defendant saith he was particular to examine when he read the said
Bond at Augusta aforesaid, because he knew his said Brother Samuel
could not read it, and because his said Brother had repeatedly told
him that he knew nothing of the contents of the Bond, only as they
read it over to him for the delivery of one negroe, and that all
the people present were Strangers to him and appeared to be his
Enemies — indeed mortal ones — he being a Prisoner and in great fear
of his life, so that the Bond might be for any thing else. To this
purport his said Bro. told him when he applied to him this Deponent
to meet the Defdt. Colhoun at Augusta to get the matter settled in
his behalf, which this Deponent saith made him very particular to
examine the said Bond when it was put into his hands at Augusta and
found it only for one negroe as his said Brother had told him, and
no credit was given on the Bond, neither were the names of Jane,
Jude and Squire mentioned in the said Bond, as this Deponent saith
he read it over and examined it very particularly.

3rd. In answer to the third Interrogatory this Deponent saith
that he believes he did request of the Defendant Colhoun a sight of
the said Bond, as his Brother Samuel had employed him to settle the
matter for him, and as he was so apprehensive that the Bond which he
had signed to the Defendant Colhoun was not a fair one, for the reasons afore mentioned, therefore this Deponent saith he wished to see
and examine the said Bond, and when he found it to be only for the
delivery of one negroe as it had been read to his Brother Saml. when
he gave it, he acknowledged the Bond to be just and assured the pay
ment of it, not only before Witnesses but he gave General Twiggs as
Security that he would deliver such a negroe as was mentioned in
the said Bond to the said Defendant Colhoun at his house in So.
Carolina by a limited time, which was done, and which his Brother
Saml. had instructed him to do, provided the Bond was a fair one,

and would be paid off with one negroe. That his said Brother Saml.
told him that altho he had never injured the said Defendant Colhoun
in any respect and altho the said Bond was extorted from him under
the greatest apprehensions of losing his life, yet he would rather
give one negroe, than to run any further risque therefore this Deponent saith thus far he was very willing to go for his said Broth
er Samuel, but the Defendant Colhoun would not at first be content
ed with this, but said that his said Bro. Samuel, the Loyds and
others had plundered a great deal of property from him, that as his
said Brother was in company he had a right to pay the whole -- that
the three negroes Jane, Jude and Squire which he had as Security
for the return of his property were now taken away, therefore he
insisted on refering the whole to an Arbitrator, to which this Deponent saith he consented, and chose General Twiggs to Arbitrate
for him in behalf of his said Brother Samuel Red, and he believes
the Defendant Colhoun chose General Pickens, but those Gentlemen
did not go into the examination of any witnesses, and they advised
us to settle our disputes ourselves. Then this Deponent saith that
the Defendant insisted that his said Brother Samuel Red ought to
pay for the three negroes Jane, Jude and Squire, which had been
taken from him by the Complainant John Lindsey, as well as the one
mentioned in the Bond, unless he would tell who was in Company
when his the said Colhouns property was plundered from him, assent
ing that he had lost more property than the whole of the four negroes were worth. But this Deponent saith that he insisted that his
said Brother Samuel knew nothing about his the said Colhouns property, nor who plundered it -- that he had never injured him in any
degree, not withstanding which this Deponent saith that he still
offered to pay off the said Bond in behalf of his said Bro. Saml.
rather than to have any further trouble about the business and
totally refused to pay any more, but still was willing to leave the
whole to an Arbitrator. This Deponent further saith that at length
the Defendant Joseph Colhoun consented to take the one negroe as
mentioned in the Bond, and he actually sent a valuable negroe boy
named Peter by the hands of Saml. Loyd, but never has been able to
get up his Brother Samuel Red's Bond, altho the Defendant Colhoun
punctually and expressly promised to send it by the person who
carried the negroe. This Deponent says he knows nothing further.
The above Deposition taken beforeus
24th Octr. 1793.   Witness our hands and Seals.
                              Isaac Perry
                              John Boutin
                              Henry Hughes

ON ANOTHER PAPER.

Burke County
State of Georgia) By virtue of a Commission issuing from the Hon-
orable Court of Equity for the District of ninety six in the State
of So. Carolina to Edward Weathers Isaac Perry, Henry Hughes, John
Bowden and Daniel Evans directed for the examination of Witnesses
in a cause there depending between John Lindsey and Robert Anderson
Complainants and Joseph Colhoun Defendant. We Issac Perry and Henry
Hughes two of the Acting Commissioners under the said commission

and also the respective Clerks by us employed in transcribing and
engrossing the said Depositors having first & severally taken the
oaths annexed to the said Commission according to the true tenor
& effect thereof and as thereby required.

On the part and behalf of the Complainants Patience Matthis
formerly Patience Loyd of the County and State aforsaid aged twenty
four years or upwards, being sick and unable to attend at the place
pointed out for taking the said Depositions, but being produced,
sworn & examined at the house of Benjamin Matthis in the State &
County aforesd on the 23d of October 1793 deposeth & saith as
follows.

1st. In answer to the first Interrogatory this Deponent saith
that she was at the house of Samuel Red about that time, when four
armed men, who were said to be from Carolina (South) came there, one
of whom said his name was Colhoun. but the names of the others she
cannot now tell. That one of the Company threatened the said Saml.
Red, they called for Victuals but told said Red that if he offered
to go away they would kill him & charged the negroes that were present not to go away & when they had eat breaksfast they ordered the
s.d Saml. Reds horse to be got that he might go along with them.
That they viz the party said they wanted Saml. Redd and his property.

2nd. In answer to the second Interrogatory this Deponent saith
that her brother Samuel Loyd was present at the house of Saml. Red
& demanded their authority, but they refused to show it. But they
did take the said Saml. Red a Prisoner & carried him away by compulsion and much agt. his the said Saml. Red's will. And they did
also take three negroes Jane, Jude & Squire out of the Possession
of Elizabeth Cartledge. Saml. Loyd & her this Deponent, who all
then lived at the house of the said Samuel Red and who were all
children & Heirs to Thomas Loyd Senr. Decesd. to whose Estate the
said three negroes did all belong. This Deponent farther saith that
she never heard of any damage or injury having been done by the
said Samuel Red to the Defendant Joseph Colhoun his family or property, except what she heard the said Colhoun and his party say at
that time.

3rd. In answer to the third Interrogatory this Deponent saith
that the said three negroes Jane Jude and Squire never did belong
to the said Samuel Red, neither did ever the said Saml. claim any
right or title in the said three negroes nor either of them, to
her this Deponents knowledge and belief. This Deponent further
saith that she believes and is well informed and persuaded that the
said Samuel Red would have opposed the Defendant Colhoun & his party
in carrying away the said three negroes (altho he claimed no right
in them) if he had been at liberty and had not been under great fear
and compulsion. That Samuel Loyd charged the said Defendant from
taking and carrying away the said three negroes & told him they were
not the right of Saml. Red but that they were the right of the
Heirs of his Fathers undivided Estate, or of him the said Saml. Loyd
as being one of the Heirs. This Deponent cannot say how the s_aid
Samuel Red was treated after he was taken from the house when he

was taken from the house when he was made Prisoner. That Samuel Red afterwards told her this Deponent that he was carried a Prisoner to Col. Clarkes by the Defendant Colhoun, who also carried the said three negroes to his Plantation in So. Carolina, but that she knows nothing of any Bond, or by what means it was obtained, or in what condition it was given.

4th. In answer to the fourth Interrogatory this Deponent saith that she knows nothing but has heard that the Complaint John Lindsey did bring back the said three negroes to Savannah River opposite Samuel Reds, as her sister Elizabeth Cartledge was sent for and Jude was brought over the River to Samuel Reds where she this Deponent lived with her said Sister Elizabeth Cartledge, but that she doth not know on what Terms, or under what restrictions the said negroes were delivered.

5th. In answer to the fifth Interrogatory this Deponent saith she knows nothing.

6th. In answer to the sixth Interrogatory this Deponent saith no, the said John Lindsey did not convert any of the said negroes to his own use, neither did he ever receive any Commission, Profit benefit or reward from the said Commissioners, to her this Deponents knowledge and belief.

7th. In answer to the seventh eighth and ninth Interrogations this Deponent saith that she might have heard something, of some of these Interrogations, but can recollect so little but this Deponent farther saith not.
The above Deposition taken before us) Witness our hands and seals 23rd October 1793.

(Note by P.Y. In the beginning the
name Bouton was written Bowden.)

Isaac Perry
John Bouton
Henry Hughes

On the part and behalf of the Defendant Joseph Colhoun, the said Patience Matthis formerly Pattience Loyd being produced, sworn and examined on the Cross Interrogatories accompanying the said Commissioner, deposeth and saith as follows.

1 & 2. In answer to the first and seconf Interrogatorys this Deponent saith, That she knows nothing about any such property being at any house nor else where, which was either said or supposed to be the property of the Defendant Colhoun. She heard that one Cooper and others had carried some property which was said to have been plundered from the Defendant Colhoun down the country and had passed near the house of Samuel Red, but she this Deponent saith that she never did see any of the said property to her knowledge and belief.

3rd. In answer to the third Interrogatory the Deponent saith that she did know three negroes named Jane, Jude and Squire which did belong to her Father Thomas Loyd Senr. Decoased in his life

tine and were left him as part of his Estate to be equally divided
among his Children and which were the very same Negroes which the
Defendant Joseph Colhoun with an armed party carried from the
House of Samuel Red when they took him a Prisioner and carried him
away, but this Deponent saith that she knows nothing of the said
Samuel Red having sold the said negroes, nor any of them to the
Defendant Colhoun, neither doth she know any thing of any damages
which had been done either by Samuel Red or the Loyds to the
Defendant Colhoun.

6th. In answer to the fourth and last Interrogatory this Deponent saith that she believes the Complainant John Lindsey did bring
back the said three negroes to Savannah River, as Jude was brought
over to Samuel Red's for Elizabeth Cartledge, but Jane and Squire
were sold to and left with Joshua Inman, by Samuel Loyd, who had
only a right to his distributive share or part of the said three
negroes, as one of the Children of her Father Thomas Loyd Senior
Deceased. however this Deponent saith that Mordciau Sheftall being
the only Surviving Executor who had qualified, and he neglecting
(which he still done) to have the Estate divided among the different Legatees, altho this deponent saith that she wrote to him &
repeatedly on the Subject, by reasons of which the said two negroes Jane and Squire still remained in the Possession of Joshua
Inman and the Heirs untill a year or two past when she obtained
possession of Squire, who is since run from her and gone back, but
saith she has commenced Suit in Law for the recovery of Jane and
her Issue, and is advised that she will recover the whole of the
said negroes viz Jane and her Children, one of whom Squire is, and
that an equal division of the sd Estate among the different Legatee
s will take place which hath been so long omitted by the negligence
of Mordceai Sheftall the acting Executor and further this Deponent
saith not.
The above Disposition taken the 23rd October 1793 before us.
                                        Isaac Perry
                                        John Bouten
                                        Henry Hughes

In Equity.
Interrogations to be administered to Daniel Butler a witness to
be produced, sworn and examined in a certain cause now pending and
at issue in the Court of Equity for the District of ninety six, in
the State of South Carolina, wherein John Lindsey and Robert Anderson are Complainants, and Joseph Colhoun Esquire is Defendant,
on the part and behalf of the Complainants.

1st. Do you know the parties, Complainants and Defendant, in
the title of these Interrogations named, or either and which of
them, and how long have you known them respectively?

2nd. Were you, or were you not present at the house of General
Elijah Clarke in Georgia, sometime on or about the 20th of September 1782 when the Defendant Joseph Colhoun, with Samuel Red, and
others came to the house of the said Genl. Clarke? If Yes, how

many were in company with the said Joseph Colhoun and Samuel Red,
did you know any, and how many of them, and what was their names?
Were they, or were they not all arrived who came in the said company, and did they, or did they not bring three negroes with them at
the same time, two wenches and a little boy, named Jane, Jude and
Squire? Was or was not the said Samuel Red considered as a prisoner
when he came there, or during the time he remained there or was he
at liberty at any time to have gone away with the property brought
with him without any hindrance, molestation or interruption of the
said Defendant Colhoun, or any of the company present. Or was, or
was not the said Samuel Red actually confined as a prisoner during
the time he remained at the house of the said General Clarke? If
yea set forth all you know of the different matters and things in
this interrogator mentioned, to the best of your knowledge remembrance & belief, fully and at large declare.

3rd. Had you formally been acquainted with the said Samuel Red,
either in person or character? Did, or did not the said Defendant
Colhoun, or anyof his Company, and which of them, inform you any
thing respecting the said Samuel Red? If Yea, what did they inform
you, and what influence had the said information upon your mind?
Were you, or were you not induced as Civil or Military officer, and
at whose request, and by whose influence, take charge of the safe
keeping of the said Samuel Red, or was he not actually confined as
a prisoner? If Yea, for what crime was he imprisoned, and who gave
you information of his crime, or who exhibited the charge against
him. Did or did not yourself, or any other person or persons in
your hearing, and who were they, use any threatening words to the
said Samuel Red, while he was a prisoner, whereby he might be put
in fear? If Yea, what were they? Set forth all you know, according
to the best of your knowledge remembrance and belief fully and at
large declare.

4th. Do you, or do you not know that Samuel Red gave a Bond to
the said Defendant Colhoun for four negroes and did he or did he
not deliver the above mentioned three negroes Jane, Jude & Squire
in part payment of the said Bond? Or did he, or did he not give
the Bond for one negroe, and did, or did the said Defend.t Colhoun
take the said three negroes, as the property of some other person
or persons, and who were they? Did or did not the said Samuel Red
voluntarily give the said Bond? Or if he had been at full liberty
to have gone away unmolested, do you believe that he would have
given the said Bond, or was it through fear & Compulsion that he
gave the said Bond, in order to save his life, or obtain his
liberty, and even the said Samuel Red set at full liberty when he
gave the said Bond, and did he not deliver the said three negroes
to the Defend.t Colhoun, or did he say that they were none of his,
and refuse to deliver them as such, and did or did not the defend
ant Colhoun send or carry away the said three negroes before he
obtained the bond from the said Samuel Red, and before the said
Red was deliberated from his imprisonment, for what purpose was he
detained a prisoner? Did the Defendant Colhoun require the delivery

of any more negroes or did he endeavour to compell any further
payment to be made by the said Samuel Red at that time, and how
afterwards did he obtain his liberty? Set forth all you know concerning the same, according to the best of your knowledge remembrance & belief and at large declare.

5th. Was it, or it not a very dangerous situation at that time
for a man to be called a Tory among a people who did not know him,
however innocent he might be, or was Tories perfectly secure at
that time in person & property untill they were legally convicted
of violating the known laws of the Country? Declare fully.

6th. Lastly, Is there any matter or thing you know or believe
to be necessary or material for the Complainants to prove in this
cause? If Yea, set forth the same, and the particular reasons &
circumstances of such your knowledge & belief, therefore fully
and at large declare.

DeSaussure
Compt. Solicitor

******

The Deposition and Examination of Daniel Butler of Wilks County
in the State of Georgia aged forty five years or there abouts a
Witness produced Sworn and Examined on the 10th Day of October
1793 at the house of James McCormick Esqr. In the State and County
Aforesaid by Virtue of a Common form Issuing from the Honourable
the Court of Equity for the District of ninety Six, in the State of
South Carolina to us James McCormick Solomon Nuson Hugh Rees John
Tarrens and Levi Pruitt Directed for the Examination of the Said
Daniel Butler, on a cause then Depending Between John Lindsey and
Robert Anderson Complainants and Joseph Colhoun Defendant we the
Said James McCormick Solomon Nuson and Hugh Rees the acting Comm-
issioners under the Said Commissioner and also the Clerk by us
Employed in Taking Transcribing & Engrossing the Said Deposition
having first Severally taken the oaths annexed to the Said Commiss
ion according to the tenor and true Effect thereof and us thereby
required. Therefore on the part & behalf of the Said Complainants
John Lindsey and Robert Anderson the Said Daniel Butler being produced Sworn and Examined on the Interrogations accompanying the
Said Commission Deposeth and Saith as follows.

1st. In answer to the first Interrogatory this Deponent saith
that he was well acquainted with the Complainant John Lindsey in
the late war and also he had repeatedly seen the Complainant
Robert Anderson and the Defendant Joseph Colhoun in the said war
but had no intimate acquaintance with Either.

2nd. In answer to the Second interrogatory this Deponent Saith
yet, he was present, that he cannot recollect that he knew any of
the Men which came with the Defendant Joseph Colhoun and Samuel
Red neither can he remember what number came in Company but there
were Several men, and he saith that to best of his remembrance

and belief they were all armed who came in Company with Red only
Red himself, that they brought with them some Negroes he believes
not less than three whose names he does not remember but he thinks
they were mostly the wenches at least two of them that Samuel Red
(as well as he can remember) was Considered a prisoner during the
time of his Stay. That the Defendant Joseph Colhoun threatened
the Said Red with him this Deponent I forming said Red that he the
Deponent had hung one Stewart a Tory Who had been lately hung ar
the end of General Clarkes lane in order to Terrify the said Red.
That altho this Deponent had not hanged Stewart as the Defendant
Colhoun and others of the Company had told Red yet this Deponent
did not Deny it to the said Red but took him and showed him at
the end of General Clarkes lane the gallows Viz. a Crooked Hickory
one which Stewart had been hanged, Assuring him the Said Red that
he must S ortly Share the same fate. That the said Samuel Red was
not at liberty to have gone away at any time during his Stay at
the house of General Clark and to the best of this Deponents know
ledge remembrance and belief the Said Red made his Escape from his
Con finement when he went away perhaps a Chance might have been
given him to Escape but he was not openly Set at liberty when he
did go to the best of this Deponents knowledge & belief.

3rd. In answer to the third Interrogatory this Deponent Saith,
That he never had heard of or had Acquaintance with the said Samuel Red or of his Caracter but the Defendant Joseph Colhoun and he
thinks Some others of the Company with him told him that Red was
a tory and a very bad man which this Deponent believed to be True,
this Deponent further Saith that he acted as Constable for General
Clark and was Still a Terror to the people called Tories and was
Considered a Killing Man and the Defendant Colhoun told this Deponent that the Said Samuel Red had plundered some of his the
Defendants property which he believed to be true and which was
Sufficient Inducement to him to do his Duty and he Considered the
orders of the Defendant & Capt. Colhoun as being a Whig officer to
be his warrant for so doing. That many threatening words were
spoken to the said Samuel Red by this Deponent and others of the
Company but he cannot remember what in particular it being so long
ago but the said Red appeared to be in great fear.

4th. In answer to the fourth Interrogatory this Deponent Saith
that as well as he can remember he heard a bond was given Samuel
Red to Colhoun but did not see the bond given or whether the bond
was for one or more negroes this Deponent saith he does not remember & thinks he never knew but as well as he can remember Samuel
Red Said that the Negroes which the Defendant Colhoun and his Company brought when they brought him were none of his right however
this Deponent Saith he only thought it a pretence and he believes
the Defendant Colhoun took or Lent off the said negroes with out
Consulting the Said Samuel Red but as whose property the Said Colhoun took the Said Negroes if he knew then he does not recollect
now but is well persuaded that if the Said Samuel Red had been at
liberty he would not have given a Bond (if he gave one at all)
but would have gone away and taken the Negroes with him, that he

does not remember whether the Defendant Colhoun required or Demanded any more from the Said Samuel Red at that time but believes Red was not Set at liberty by the Defendant Colhoun but afterwards made his Escape.

5th. In answer to the fifth Interrogatory this Deponent saith that the name of Tory at that time was Sufficient condemnation and there was no legal conviction required in Wilks County only Sufficient Testimony that they were Tories and the (word not plain) of a known reputable Whig was Sufficient for that purpose.

6th. In answer to the Sixth Interrogatory this Deponent Saith that on or about the 28th day September last he was under an agreement to meet his Brother at the widow Barbson's South about 18 miles from his own house and according to promise met him there who told this Deponent that the Defendant Colhoun was then over about this business and that if this Deponent would befriend him in giving his Evidence that if the Deponent wanted money or any thing Else it would not be lacking this Deponent Saith that he replyed to his Brother that he Supposed the Defendant Colhoun might be a good man but that he this Deponent did not want to see him as was Determined to Swear to nothing, but the truth according to his best recollection when ever Called upon in the business. This Deponent further Saith that the next morning he set out on his return home and the Defendant Colhoun rode with him near ten miles & had much Conversation Lamenting this Deponents Situation in having been wounded in the Wars and told him this Deponent that as they did not do him further Justice in Georgia by allowing him an annuity that if he would come over to Carolina that he might make his house his home it Should not Cost him this Deponent one farthing & that he should not want for money and that then he could attend Court to give Evidence on this Case this Deponent further saith that the Defendant Colhoun Said much to him upon the Subject of his Law suit with the Complainant John Lindsey it Cheifly took up the whole of the Conversation while they rode near ten miles and the defendant Colhoun during the time repeatedly pressed this deponent to go with him to Squire McCormicks and Swear before him that what he could recollect about this business at length this Deponent told the Defendant Colhoun that he would not go to Squire McCormicks at that time or Swear anything about the matter but if he did not go to Court he assured him if he was Sworn here by Commission he would Swear to nothing but the truth and so parted from the Defendant Colhoun and Further this Deponent Saith not.

ON ANOTHER PAPER.

Wm. Hutchinson lives about a half a mile from Col. Colhoun. Thre 18 years., he was plundered by unknown persons about the time that Col. C. was plundered. Also states that Red was tryed by a court and sentenced to give the bond to Col. Colhoun for the delivery of 3 negroes or be hanged in 10 days.... Mr. Pettigrew. In Sept. 1782 he was stationed in a block house near Genl. Pickens & Capt. Col-

houn was there, that he mentioned to me his going into the state
of Georgia some time after my self & others met at the House of
sd. Colhoun, we moved on to Georgia to the House of Pain on Little
River, we had arms, from there we went below Augusta. We went to
Reds house on monday morning and Red stepped to the door. Mr. Colhoun asked him who lived there. Red told him he did, upon which
Calhoun told him he was glad to see him, there were three in the
party besides Calhoun who all dismounted. Calhoun accused Red of
being accessory of carrying off his property of his which Red
denied. Calhoun told him that that if he could not prove that Red
was accessory to taking his property he should not be hurt. We
breaksfasted and immediately after breakfastCalhoun purposed in
taking 2 negro girls & 1 Boy and ordered me to take Red a prisoner
on which I clapped him on the shoulder and took Red a prisoner,
we then proceeded on towards Augusta, the woman who Red called his
wife, or said to be Reds wife came to the Road & proposed a Mr.
Inman to be Reds security. Mr. Calhoun proposed to go on very
slow and if the had a mind to overtalk as they might, we proceed
on towards Augusta and met some Gentlemen Col. Jackson was one
who ast us what authority the negroes were taken, Col. Calhoun
handed a paper to Col. Jackson out of his pocket which Jackson
say.d was good, we went next morning to Augusta where Col. C.
stoped some time, next 'day proceeded to the Kiscas about 20 miles
and lodged at one Cilgores & from thence to Colo. Clarks, Reds
House 20 miles below Augusta. We came to Clarks on thursday or
friday, that day I left them and went to Capt. Calhoun. Calhoun
wished the party to behave very peacible, and said that if he
could not prove that Red was the man who pludered him, that he &
his property should be free, the reason for that, the negroes to
Clark as given by Calhoun was that the witnesses lived there.
Red was never confined close. A young woman at Reds claimed one
of the negroes. Question. Did you see a Mr. Butler at Clarks.
Answer. Saw a small man who he does not know that his name was
Butler. The two Davises that were of the Party were peacible
honest men. ... Capt. Calhoun commanded at the Block House...
Alexander Davis sworn, I was doing a tour of duty with Mr. Pettigrew at the block House where Capt. Calhoun commanded. Calhoun
came to me and requested me to go with him to Georgia in pursuit
of some property that was plundered from him. I went with him to
the House of Red. Pettigrew went, Red was in the yard & Pettigrew
spoke first and ask Red if he acknowledged himself a prisoner.
Col. Calhoun then spoke to Red and ask him his name which he told
himwas Sam Red Red was not delivered into Butlers Custody while at
Clarkes. . We traveled the public road from Reds very slow as the
negroes were on foot. There was not at this time any Court of
Justice...

Other notes of interest from the above paper, Little River from
Augusta was about 28 miles.

Isaac Matthews sworn, In the year 1782 in September at Genl.
Clarks house where I met Calhoun, he told me to take notice, that
were 2 or 3 negroes in the house, that they did not run away,

after some time a Mr. Paine came. I had seen Red previous to
Pains coming. Pain & Red walked off together several rods and
conversed, after sometime they returned & Colo. Cunningham, ...
Walton & Geo. Dooley came up & went into the house, Calhoun was
then talking to Pain & Red came to them & told him Calhoun that
he was willing to make it up, Col. Cunningham, Walton & Dooley
went into a side room & they talked concerning negroes, Calhoun
prop osed to Red that if he would take his oath concerning the
matter that he would discharge him & his property, Red answered
that he would rather pay than swear anything about it. Colo.
Cunningham answered that one rouge hated to swear against another,
a great deel was then said concerning a B nd, and a Bond was
drawn by Walton. The Bond was then produced & acknowledged, he
heard the Bond read in presence of Red. A Mr. Loyd was there and
went from the house with Red & conversed privately, Loyd took a
paper out of his pocket & gave it to Paine, he heard Red acknow
ledge the woman in the house to be his wife..... Wm. Hays sworn,
I went to Calhouns & there I saw Major Lindsey & others standing
before the door. Calhoun was not at home, I went for him to a
neighbors house, when he returned Lindsey told him he had come
for the negroes. Calhoun asked him if they were confiscated, Lind
sey told him they were & took some papers out of his pocket and
selected one from the rest which Lindsey said was his authority,
it was notoriously known that Lindsey was a Commissioner, Linddsey
told Calhoun that he should be paid, that the public negroes were
hired out, that in a short time they would be called in and sold
to pay public debts. Calhoun asked Lindsey to leave the Property
with him and he would give Gen. Prather? as security in the State
& in Georgia from Gen. Clark. Lindsey told him he could not answer for his conduct to the B. of Commissioners for his taking
security. Lindsey told him the negroes he would have unless he
was prevented by force of arms, both Parties till now appeared to
be mild, but that this deponent recommended Calhoun to give up
the Negroes. After dinner Lindsey went to the negroes & ordered
then to prepare themselves to go with him, the negroes made ready.
Patrick Calhoun sworn, that in the year 1782 Major Lindsey towards
the evening od a day came to my house and a number of negroes
with him, he told me the matter concerning the negroes that
Calhoun & Lindsey could not agree about the delivery of the Negroes... Ben. Howard sworn, I & Col. Anderson in the spring 88
was at Mr. Leslies and there understood that he got the better
of Col. Calhoun in law the first tryal. Col. Anderson said that
Calhoun had come to him in a friendly manner that he would assist
him in getting his money, but now he would oppose him... Wm.
Hutton sworn, In the year 91 in the last of Nov or the 1 of Dec.
I was in Augusta he met M. Lindsey in Hunt & Hattons?store. Mr.
Lindsey said he would always support Col. Anderson in a legal
suit, but if otherwise he would not... Mr. Forunan? sworn, A
paper presented to know of Mr. Forunan? wether he saw it sign?
he knew the hand writin Mr. Forunan says that Butler is a man
of indifferent character, that he was convicted before a Justice
for theft - Pain is considered as an honest man but a Tory. Mr.
G. Walton was a Justice of the peace, Cunningham was a honest

character, he does not conceive that Mr. Cunningham or Mr. Walton
would have suffered a Bond to be extorted on their prisoner, they
were both Magistrates. Col. Clark was never a magistrate neither
was Butler ever a Constable, Butler happened to call at his house
& ask, what had become of this Suit, and expressed a wish in
favor of Calhoun. Freeman? he lived in Georgia in B. there was
very little law, but justices of the peace did some business. Col.
Clark was violent in arms. ... Mr. Dunlap sworn, I was appointed
an arbitrator by Lindsey by reason that Calhoun was his neighbor,
but could not get off... Major Taylor sworn, In 1783 he was in
Augusta when he saw a man by the name of Red. Genl. Pickens & he
were together, that Calhoun sd. he wanted them to be present at
a transaction that a Bond was produced read & that Genl.Twiggs
sd that Red was an honest man but that his Brother Sam Red was a
dam.d Raskel, that Red came to Calhoun to settle the Ballance of
the Bond.

One paper stated that St. Georges Parish was now Burke County as
well as on Little River, then Richland County.... John Cunningham
Esquire was of Elbert County, Georgia.

To whom it may concern. These Calhoun papers are locked in the
vault in the Clerks Office, any one visiting there, should ask
him for permisssion to see them. The reason why no number is
given to this package. P.Y.

URSLEY JOHNSON TO JOHN LONGERDS
DEED PACK. 498
CLERK OF COURTS OFFICE, ABBEVILLE, S.C.

St. of South Carolina
Abbeville Dist.

Know all men by these Presents that I Ursley Johnson of the Dist. and
State afore Said For and in consideration of the Sum of one hundred
Dollars to in hand Paid by John Longerds Have granted bargained Sold
and Released and by these Presents do grant bargain Sell and Release
unto the Said John Longerds a certain track or parcel of land contain
ing Nine acres lying and being in the dist afore Said It being Part
of track of land which I bought of William Burton its lying N E Side
of the main road from Pendleton to Charleston and hath Such marks
buting and bounding as in the Plat thereunto anext together with all
and Singular the rights Members hereditments and appertenances to the
Said Premises belonging or in any wise incident or Apertaining to
have and to hold all and the Premises before mentioned Unto the Said
John Longerds his heirs and assigns for ever and I do hereby Bind my
Self my heirs Executors administrators to John Longerds his heirs and
assigns against myself and against my heirs and against every Person
whom So ever lawfully claiming or to claim the Same or any Part there
of in witness where of I have here unto Set my hand and Seal this
September the 26th, 1809, in the year of our lord one thousand Eight
hundred and nine
Signed Sealed and Delivered in the Presents of

	her
Robert Page or Pope?	Ursley X Johnson (LS)
William Langerds	mark
James Langerds	

(Name written Longerds & Langerds. No recording date given.)

. . . .

JOSEPH H. SANDERS & OTHERS TO JOHN ADAMS
PACK. 499   DEED
CLERK OF COURTS OFFICE, ABBEVILLE, S.C.

The State of South Carolina
Know all men by these presents that we Joseph Hall Sanders, Wm.
Springle & Frances Springle his wife, and Marcus D. Moore & Catharine
his wife, heirs & devisees of Joseph Sanders late of Abbeville district deceased, and heirs & distributees of John Sanders decd. one of
the joint devisees of the said Joseph Sanders, & heirs & distributees
of Rebecca Sanders the widow & relict of the Said Joseph Sanders &
mother of the said Joseph Hall Sanders, Frances Springle & Catharine
Moore, of Marengo County in the State of Alabama, in consideration of
the sum of six hundred & five dollars to us paid by John Adams of Abbe'
ville district in the State of South Carolina, have granted, bargained,
sold & released, and by these presents do grant, bargain sell & release

unto the said John Adams all that tract of land late the property of
Joseph Sanders dec.d containing one hundred & ninety three acres and
four chains, more or less, situate in Abbeville district aforesaid
on McCords creek & Long Cane, bounded by lands of James Wardlaw, Mrs
Tennent & Wm P Paul, & having such artificial & natural descriptive
marks as a plat thereof, hereto annexed, represents, together with
all and singular the rights, members, hereditaments and appertenances
to the said premises belonging or in any wise incident or appertaining, to have & to hold all and singular the premises before mentioned,
unto the said John Adams, his heirs & assigns forever. And we do here
by bind ourselves, our heirs, executors and administrators, to warrant and forever defend, all & singular the said premises unto the
said John Adams, his heirs and assigns, against ourselves and our
heirs, and against every person whomsoever, lawfully claiming or to
claim the same as any part there of.

     Witness our hands and seals this twenty third day of March in
the year of our Lord one thousand eight hundred & thirty one and in
the fifty fifth year of the independence of the United States of
America.

Signed sealed & delivered in	Joseph H Sanders (LS)
presence of	William Springle (LS)
by Jos H. Sanders	Frances Springle (LS)
A. Bowie	M.D. Moore (LS)
D Lesly	Catharine Moore (LS)

Executed by Wm. Springle & wife
& M.D. Moore & wife
in presence of
Wm. T. Linson
Julius Norton

South Carolina
Abbeville District) I David Lesly do solemnly swear that I was personally present and did see Jos H Sanders Sign, Seal and as his act
and deed deliver the within release for the use & purpose therein
mentioned and that A Bowie with myself in the presence of each other
witnessed the execution of the same. Sworn to before me the 26 June
1839.

                Jno F Livingston
                Clk & Ex off Qm.

The State of Alabama
Marengo County) We R.R. Moore & Daniel T. Fitchett, Commissioners
duly empowered in & by virtue of the annexed Dedimuspotestatem, do
hereby certify unto all whom it may concern that, Frances Springle
the wife of the within named named Wm. Springle, and Catharine Moore,
the wife of the within named Marcus D. Moore, did this day appear be
fore us, and upon being privately & seperately examined by us, did
declare that each of them, for herself, did at least seven days before
the time of such examination actually join her husband in executing
the within release, and that she did then and each of them does now
freely voluntarily & without any manner of compulsion, dread or fear

of any person or persons whomsoever, renounce, release & forever re-
linquish all her estate, interest & inheritance in the premises mentioned in the within release, unto the within named John Adams & his
heirs & assigns. And that the within release was postively & bona fide
executed more than seven days before this examination.

  Given under our hands & seals this Eleventh day of November Anno
domini 1831.
Daniel T. Fitchett Justice Peace (LS) Frances Springle (LS)
R.R. Moore Justice Peace (LS) Cathern Moore (LS)

Alabama — Marengo County — I swear that I was present & Saw Marcus D.
Moore & Catharine his wife, & Wm. Springle & Frances his wife, sign
seal & as their act & deed deliver the within deed to & for the uses,
intents & purposes therein mentioned and that William T. Lintson with
me witnessed the due execution thereof.
Daniel T. Fitchett Justice Peace   Julius Norton
R.R. Moore Justice Peace

      •

       BASDALL DARBY TO JOHN ADAMS
       PACK. 500 DEED
       CLERK OF COURTS OFFICE, ABBEVILLE, S.C.

State of South Carolina Abbeville District
Know all men by these presents that I basdal Darby for the inconsider
ation of the sum of twelve hundred & twenty Dollars to me in hand paid
by John Addams of S.d State & District afore S.d have granted bargained
& Sold & by these presents Dow grant bargain & Sell & relese unto the
a bove named John Addams all that Track of Land or plantation Contain-
ing two hundred & twenty five acres more or Less situate in the State
& District afore s.d being a track of Land originally granted to robt
Norras Jur. also part of a track of Land orignley be Longing to John
Foster Decest Ling on Frazars Creek waters of Norris Creek waters of
Long Cane Creek bonded by John fosters Land & by Thos Ousburn Land &
on the North by E C Morgans Land and has Such Shape & bounding & marks
as the two plats will more fullyplanly represent together with all and
Singular the rights members hereditments & apertance to the Sd premises
be Longing or in any wise Men Dent or appertaning to have & to hold all
and Singler the premises before mentioned unto the Sd John Adams his he
heirs and assigns for ever & the S.d basdal Darby Do bind my Self my
heirs & executors administrators to warrant and for ever Defend all &
Singular the sd premises andtoothevSd DohnAdaik hislhghlar& asigns
for ever aganst my Self my heirs exutors & administrators and every
pther pursons hume so ever Lawfully Claiming or to Claim the Same or
any part thare of witness my hand and Sele this twenty third Day of
October in the year of our Lord one thousan eight hundred and twenty
two and in the forty Six year of the independence of amerácha
Signed Sealed in presents of
Sam L Watt   Basdall Darby (LS)
Thos. McMillion

South Carolina
Abbeville District) I John Devlin one of the Justices Quorum do here
by certify unto all whom it may concern that Martha Darby wife of the
within named Basdal Derby did this day appear before me & upon being
privately & separately examined by me did declare that she does free
ly voluntarily & without any compulsion dread or fear of any person
or persons whomsoever renounce release & forever religuish unto the
within named John Adams his heirs & assigns all her interest & estate
&also all her right & claim of dower of in or to all & singular the
premises within mentioned & released.

Given under my hand & seal 15th day of March 1823.

(LS) John Devlin   Martha Darby

The State of Mississippi
Pontotoc? County)   Personally appeared before me Benj D Anderson a
Justice of the peace in & for Said County the within named Saml. L
Watt one of the Subscribing witnesses to the within deed, who being
first duly sworn deposeth and Saith that he Saw the within named
Basdail Darby whose name is Subscribed thereto sign seal and deliver
the same to the within named John Adams, that he this deponent Subs-
cribed his name as a witness thereto in the presence of the said
Basdail Darby, and that he Saw the other Subscribing witness Thos.
McMillian Sign the Same in the presence of the S.d Basdail Darby and
in the presence of each other on the day and year therein named.

Given under my hand & Seal the 15th day of October 1838.
                              Benj. D. Anderson (LS)
                              Justice of the peace

. . . .

ESTATE OF BELINDA CALDWELL, PACK. 3350
BILL FOR ACCOUNT & RELIEF
CLERK OF COURTS OFFICE, ABBEVILLE, S.C.

South Carolina
Abbeville District) To the Honorable the Chancellors of the said State.
    Humbly complaining shew unto your Honors your oratrix Belinda Cald-
well, that heretofore on the day of June in the year of our Lord one
thousand eight hundred and twenty Six Hugh P rter was appointed by this
Honorable Court guardian of the person and property of your oratrix.
That as your oratrix is informed and verily believes the said Hugh
Porter as guardian of your oratrix, received from the estate of her
deceased father John Caldwell several large sums of money, which with
the interest thereon are now in his hands. That the expenditures by the
said Hugh P rter in behalfof your oratrix have been exceedingly small,
and that now in sum of money considerably greater thanthe original fund
of your oratrix, is in the possession of the said Hugh Porter, for which
which he refuses to account with your oratrix.

To the end therefore that the said Hugh guardian as aforesaid may in
full and perfect manner make to the matters and things herein before
set forth, and that the said Hugh Porter may be decreed and ordered
by this Honorable Court to account for, and pay over to your oratrix
Belinda Caldwell the sums of money, and funds he received from the
estate of John Caldwell deceased in behalf of your oratrix, with the
increase of said funds and come to a final settlement with your
oratrix, touching said funds, and for such other and further relief
as to your Honors shall deem meet.

May it please your Honors to grant unto your oratrix the writ of
subpoena to be directed to the said Hugh Porter requiring him to
answer this bill agreeably to Law and the practice of this Honorable
Court, and to abide such decree therein as to your Honors shall deem
agreeable to Equity and good Conscience.

And your oratrix will ever pray &c.

Filed the 4th April 1839.

Burt & Thomson
Comp. Sol.

May 10-1843 Mr. Thompson Dear Sir
   at the request of Mr. Porter I write you a line he has taken
Belinda home with him I have no objections to his remaining her guardian and to let the business rest in his hand, to give him time to make
his arangments more Satisfactorly as he says he was ignorant of her
nessesitys and that he will provide for her untill he gets her guardianship Setled I as myself have no disposion to have him forced into
measures that would distress him
                              D. H. Cochran

Apl 12-1844 Mr. Thompson
Dear Sir this is to inform you that the case of Belinda Caldwell
angainst Hugh Porter is so near settled that I have reason to believe
it will be amicably Setled and wish the case to be stoped at what it
is at and let her money remain in his hands as her guardian and consider the case Setled   D. H. Cochran

May 7th 1844 Mr Thompson
Dear sir this comes to inform you that I am willing for you to say the
case Belinda Calwell against Hugh Porter is Setled for I am Satisfied f
for it to so Yours with respect   her
                                    Belinda X Caldwell
                                          mark

Mr Thompson this comes to inform you that I am willing that you should
stop your proceedings in the case Belinda Caldwell against Hugh Porter
and let my money remain in his hands and be paid out as I may need as
I am liveing with him at present Yours with respect May 11th 1845
Test   her
Willison F B Porter   Belinda X Calwell
                                          mark

April 1st 1844 Dear Sir ater my respects to you this comes to inform

you that I am willing that you should mark the case Belinda Caldwell
against Hugh Porter Settled and let whatever may be comeing to her re
main in his hands and be paid out as she may need as I am disposed to
believe he will do what is right

William Caldwell

April 2nd 1844 after my respects to you this comes to inform you that
I am willing that I am willing (note by P.Y. written twice) that you
should mark the case Belinda Caldwell against Hugh Porter setled and
let the whatever may be comeing to remain in his hands and be paid
out as she may need as I am disposed to believe he will do what is
right
Mr Thompson   Benjamin Adams

. . . .

ESTATE OF JOHN STEPHENS   PACK. 3351
BILL FOR SPECIFIC PERFORMANCE
CLERK OF COURTS OFFICE, ABBEVILLE, S.C.

The State of South Carolina
Abbeville District)   In Equity.
To the Honorable the Chancellors of the said State.
Humbly complaining sheweth unto your Honors your orator John Robertson as follows. About the 21st day of October in the year of our Lord
one thousand eight hundred and thirty nine John Stephens late of Abbeville District now deceased sold to your orator parcels of land
known as the surveys of John Scott lying on Willson's Creek containing
about four hundred acres more or less which your orator in pursuance
of the said agreement entered upon immediately, and now has in his
possession.
     And the said John Stephens on his part undertook and promised
your orator to give him good and lawful titles to the same as soon as
your orator should pay or cause to be paid the purchase money of the
said parcels of land.The purchase money was three thousand dollars
to be paid in three annual instalemnts on the first days of January
1840 1841 and 1842, all which will more fully appear by reference to
a copy of said agreement herewith filed and marked exhibit "A".

     About the 6th of July Anno Domini one thousand eight hundred and
forty one, and before all the purchase money was paid, their being
still one instalment unpaid, and consequently before titles were executed according to the said agreement the said John Stephens departed
this life intestate leaving as his heirs and distributees his widow
Mary M Stephens and one child Sarah Jane Stephens of very tender years.

     Administration of the estate of the said John Stephens has been
granted by the ordinary of the said District to Robert Davis Esq. At
the time of his death of the said John Stephens your orator had paid
all the purchase money but one instalment being one thousand dollars,
which he has since paid to Robert Davis the administrator of the
estate of the said John Stephens and he is now desirous of having good

titles executed to him according to the said agreement.

In tender consideration whereof and for as much as your orator is remindiless save by the aid of this Honorable Court where such matters are properly cognizable and reliable. To the end therefore that the said Mary M. Stephens Sarah Jane Stephens and Robert Davis may upon their several corporal oaths full true and perfect answer make in the premises as fully as if the same were here repeated and they thereunto specially interrogated that insuch way as to your Honors may seem proper titles, may be made to your orator of the land aforesaid, and that your orator may have such other and further relief as may be agreeable to Equity and good consceience.

May it please your Honors to grant to your orator your writ of subpoena directed to the said Mary M. Stephens, Sarah Jane Stephens & Robert Davis, requiring them, on a day certain to be and appear in this Honorable Court and to abide and perform such order and decree in the premises as to your Honors may seem meet and your orator will ever pray &c.

Filed 2 Nov. 1843.

Perrin & McGowan
Com. Sol.

BOND FOR TITLES.

The State of South Carolina
Abbeville District)   Know all men by these presents that I John Stephens of the District of Abbeville and State of South Carolina of the one part and John Robertson of the other part witnesses that I John Stephens doth obligate and bind myself my heirs Executors assigns and administrators in a bond of six thousand dollars to make the said John Robertson his heirs Executors assigns and administrators certain deeds to pieces or parcels of land lying on Wilsons creek known by the surveys of John Scott, left to the said John Stephens and to Thomas Scott the husband of Elisabeth Scott for which I John Stephens am to make or cause to be made sufficient titles to the above mentioned lands to the said J Robertson himself, his heirs Executors assigns or administrators forever to warrant and defend against all other claims against the said lands for which I John Robertson am to pay to the said John Stephens the sum of three thousand dollars for the above mentioned tract of land to be paid in three equal payments say the first day of January Eighteen hundred and forty January forty one January forty two

Also be it known that the effect of the said bond is to show a bargain existing between the above mentioned parties that they are equally bound them selves their heirs Executors assigns and administrators and of the above bond be complyed with it is to be null and void if not to remain in full force in law given under our hands and seals this 21st of October 1839
sealed signed and delivered in the presence of
John W. Brown
Nancy C. Bowie   John Stephens (LS)

The State of South Carolina
Abbeville District) To the Honorable the Judges of the Court of
Equity of the said State.

    Humbly complaining Sheweth unto your Honors your orator John Young
and your oratrix Mary Young his wife. That John Bickett late of Abbeville District on or about the   day of in the year of our Lord one
thousand eight hundred and three or four departed this life intestate
seized and possessed at the time of his death of a considerable real
and personal estate, leaving a widow Nancy Bickett the mother of your
oratrix Mary and the following children (viz) Jenny Bickett and Mary
Bickett and another who died an infant shortly after the death of the
Intestate. Your orator and oratrix further shewruhhe your Honors that
Nancy Bickett the widow administrated upon the estate of the Said Intestate in the same year that he died and took possession of the personal estate to a considerable amount perhaps of the value of seven or
eight hundred dollars or other large amount and eithersold or disposed of the same. Your orator and oratrix further shew unto your
Honors that the said Nancy died intestate the same year that her husband the intestate departed this life and that upon her death Joseph
Creswell Senr. took into his own hands & possessed himself of the said
personal estate or of the monys & notes & other accounts which were
taken for the sale of the Same. Your orator John Young further shews
unto your Honors that on or about the   day of July one thousand
eight hundred and sixteen he intermarried with your oratrix Mary
Bickett now Mary Young.Your orator and oratrix further shews unto
your Honors that the real estate of the said Intestate John Bickett
consisted of a tract of land containing one hundred and twenty acres
more or less lying in the district of Abbeville on Long Cane Creek
and that the Said Joseph Creswell went into possession thereof upon
the death of Nancy the mother of your oratrix Mary Young about the
year one thousand eight hundred and three or four & has continued in
possession of said land ever since up to the present time and has
received large rents and profits from the same every year. During all
which period your oratrix Mary was a minor & incapable of attending
to her own affairs. Your orator and oratrix further shew unto your
Honors that they are informed and believe that the said John Bickett
in his life sold a horse for the sum of one hundred Dollars to a certain Moses McCarter & took his note with good security which said note
fell into the hands of the said Joseph Creswell Senr. who by neglect
& indulgence to the parties suffered it to be lost by the (word not
plain, P.Y.) of said parties whereas if it had been pursued in time it
might have been recovered. Yourorator and oratrix further shew unto
your Honors that they have often applied to the said Joseph Creswell
Senr. in a friendly manner and desired him to give your orator or
oratrix an account of the personal estate of the said Intestate John
Bickett and also an account of the rents issues & profits of the said
land and that he might pay over to your orator & oratrix what upon
such account should appear to be due to them in right of your oratrix,
and your orator and oratrix well hoped that the Said Joseph Creshh
have complied with such their reasonable requests as in justice &

Equity he ought to have done. But now so it is may it please your
Honors, that the said Joseph refuses to give or render to your orator
and oratrix any account whatsoever of the said Inteste's personal
estate or of the rents issues & profits of his real estate. In tender
consideration whereof & for as much as matters of this nature are re-
mediable only in a Court of Equity and in regard that your orator &
oratrix cannot compel the said Joseph to account for the said intestates personal estate and the rents profits and issues of his real
estate without the assistance of this Honorable Court. To the End there
fore that the said Joseph Creswell Senr. may upon his corporal oath
true and perfect answer make to all and Singular the premises as fully
& particularly as if the same were again repeated & intended. And that
the Said Joseph Creswell may be decreed to come to a just & fair account with your orator and oratrix for the personal estate of the said
John Bickett and for the rents issues and profits of his real estate
and that he may pay to your orator & oratrix what upon Such amount
shall appear to be due to them. And that your orator and oratrix may
have such other and further relief in the premises as to your Honors
shall seem meet.

May it please your Honors to grant unto orator and oratrix the
writ of Subpoena to be divided to the said Joseph Creswell Senr. there
by commanding him at a certain day and under certain penalty therein
to be inserted, personally to be and appear before your Honors in this
Honorable Court then and there to answer the premises & to attend to &
abide such order and decree therein as to your Honors shall deem meet
& agreeable to Equity and good consecience.
And your orator & oratrix shall ever pray &c.

                                                     Noble
Filed 12th April 1820.   Compt. Solr.

EXPENDITURES OF THE ESTATE OF JOHN BICKETT.

Oct. 1803	To cash paid A. Hamilton Ordinary his fees.	5/12/5
Apl. 18, 1804	Cash paid Thos. Gray his acct. £2.9.10½.	10/70/0
	Cash paid for two coffins & nails	3/00/00
	Cash pd. J. Patterson for drawing titles	1/00/0
Sept. 12.	Cash paid David Pressly as pr. Acct.	3/69/0
	Cash paid Hugh McCormick prin. & Int.	65/16/0
Sept. 14	Cash paid Saml Glasgow	3/00/0
Oct. 8	Cash pd. Jas. Wardlaw Clerk	50/0
	Cash paid James Cooper as pr. Rect.	6/00/0
	Cash paid John Leard proven acct.	3/00/0
	Cash paid Josiah Patterson his act.	18/13/8
1805 May 1	Cash paid Abel Jackson principal and interest of a note of hand	131/35/9
	Cash before paid A. Jackson time not recollected by the hands of T.Mitchell	20/00/0
	Cash paid Saml. Young his acct.	50/0
1806 Apl. 17	Cash pd. Agnes McFarland pr. rect.	33/63/0
Oct. 20	Pd. A. Hamilton ordinaries fees pr rect.	5/91/0
	Cash pd. at different times to John Caldwell in the case od David Bickett vs. J. Creswell	95/64/5

The State of South Carolina
Abbeville District) To the honorable the Judges of the Court of Equity
of the said state.
    Humbly complaining sheweth unto your honors your orator Polly Stew-
art of the district & State aforesaid by Ezekiel Leeopard(note by P.Y.
am not postive of the spelling of Leeopard as the name was badly
written) that she is the wife of William Stewart, of the same state &
district aforesaid, by lawful marriage. That she has always entertained
a due sense of her matrimonial obligations, and in every particular has
endeavored to discharge with fidelity the various duties of her station.
For a short period after her intermarriage with the said William, she
was favored with all the happiness attendant on a union of this nature.
But the harsh & untoward disposition of the said William soon discovered itself in acts of oppression & cruelty too outrageous to be borne
and almost too shocking to be told. At various times & without any provocation he beat & abused your orator until to relieve herself from his
blows, she was compelled to leave his house & seek refuge in the
charity of some relatives or friend. At last however on one occasion, he
beat her with so much severity that she was unable to leave the house,
when the said William went away himself, taking with him every article
of value about the house, except a bed and leaving your orator with out
one mouthful of food of any description. Being left in this condition,
after a few days by the advice of her friends, she removed to her
fathers house where she found a home & protection until the said William, from some motive unknown to your orator, consented to permit her
to live in the house from which she had been driven (the said Wm. having
taken his residence elsewhere) and to furnish her with meat & bread and
the milk of one cow. With this humble support she was satisfied, & but
for the fear that even this would be denied her, she would never have
appealed to extraordinary powers of this Court. But such is the in
human and savage indifference of the said William, that, as your Orator
is informed & verily believes, the said William has sold his land & is
about to remove with his other property to the State of Alabama or some
other place beyond the limits of this State, thus depriving your orator
of the slender pittance which he has hitherto allowed her, and leaving
her without a home, dependant for Subsistence before her own exertions
and the charity of poor relations. Your orator further Complaining
sheweth unto your honors, that not with standing the unkind & abusive
conduct of the said William, she has repeatedly proposed to him that
she would return to the discharge of her marital duties if he would
permit her & give her the protection & humane treatment due to her sex, but
but this he as often & absolutely refused, swearing he would never live
with her again. Thus situated she has no hope of future reconciliation,
& to follow him in his removal would be little better than an act of
madness. Your orator further sheweth unto your honors that the said
William although a poor man is nevertheless able & she presumes un
questionably bound to yield her such support & maintenance as will be
consistment with the amount of his property. A home, which she could
call her own, if but an acre of ground, would satisfy desires which she
be Sitated not to over have no unreasonable scope. Her life has been

one of industry, and her hands can supply all her humble wants. The
said William was possessed in his own right when your oratrix was driven
from his protection of a tract of land containing about one hundred &
seventy acres of good quality, a valuable negro man & a good stock of
horses, cattle &c. and a reasonable proportion of other property common
in families of similiar rank. But of this property your orator now
claims a reasonable support. In tender consideration whereof & for as
much as your orator is remediless save in this honorable Court. To the
end therefore, that the said Wm. Stewart may upon his oath true & perfect
ect answer make to the premises in as full a manner as if the same
were here again repeated & be thereto specially interrogated, and that
he may be decreed to secure to your orator a fair & reasonable allowance
for maintenance & support, and be restrained from removing himself &
his property beyond the limits of this state until the order & decree
of this Court in the premises shall be done & performed and that your
orator may have such further & other relief in the premises as to your
honors shall seem meet. May it please your honors to grant to your
oratrix your writ of Ne Exeat to restrain the said Wm. from removing
himself or his property beyond the limits of this state & also your
writ of Subponea requiring the said Wm. to answer the premises &c. requiring your orator will ever pray &c.

                                        A. Bowie
Filed 7th Sept. 1820.   Comp. Sol.

. . . .

                ESTATE OF THOMAS GRAY   PACK. 3354
                BILL FOR PARTITION
                CLERK OF COURTS OFFICE, ABBEVILLE, S.C.

South Carolina
Abbeville District) To the Honorable the Judges of the Court of Equity
in the State aforesaid.

    Humbly complaining, your oratrix Sarah Gray of the District of Abbe-
ville and State aforesaid. Sheweth unto your honors that Thomas Gray
late of the district and State aforesaid died intestate on the   day
of   leaving your oratrix his widow and relict, and five minor children to wit, Elizabeth, Mary, Margaret & Sarah Gray. That the said Thos-
mas Gray was at the time of his death seized and possessed of in fee,
of a plantation or tract of land containing about   acres Situate
in the district aforesaid on Long Cane Creek, waters of Savannah River,
bounded by lands of James Gray, Thomas Creswell, Edward Collier & James
Goodwin one third part of which, by the act of distribution of this
State, descended to your oratrix, and the balance to the children above
mentioned share & share alike.
    In tender consideration whereof and for as much as the said minors
and from their tender years incapable of consenting to a partition of
the said tract of land, except under the direction of this honorable
court. To the end therefore that the said Elizabeth, William, Mary,
Margaret & Sarah may by themselves or their guardian true and perfect
answer make to all and singular the matters and things aforesaid, and

that a writ of partition may issue from this court directed to fit a
proper person, therein to be named requiring to divide & make partition of the premises above mentioned, among all the parties interested,
or to recomend a sale of the premises & distribution of the proceeds,
agreeably- to the act of Assembly in such case made & provided, and that
your oratrix may such other & farther relief as to your shall seem meet.

May it please your honors to grant your writ of Subpoena to be dir-
ectedthe said defendants, requiring them on a certain day to appear in
this court to answer the premises aforesaid, and to stand to and abide
by such order and decree in the premises as seem to your honors agree
able to Equity and good consecience.

And your oratrix will ever pray &o.

                                        McCraven
FiledJune 11, 1821.   Com. Sol.

. . . .

                ESTATE OF JOHN MOORE PACK. 3355
                BILL FOR PARTITION
                CLERK OF COURTS OFFICE, ABBEVILLE, S.C.

South Carolina
Abbeville District) To the Honorable Henry W. Desaussure, Theodore
Gaillard, Thomas Waters? (not postive of the name Waters,P.Y.) William
D. James and Waddy Thompson Esquires, Judges of the Court of Equity for
the State aforesaid. Humbly complaining your orator William Alexander
of the District of Abbeville and State aforesaid, Sheweth unto your
honors. That John Moore late of the District and State aforesaid, died
intestate on the day of   1814, leaving Jemima Moore his widow and
relict and three minor children to wit Thomas Lewis Moore, Jeremiah
Edwin Moore, and John Singleton Moore. That the said John Moore was at
the time of his death seized and possessed in fee of a valuable plant
ation containing about two hundred acres, Situate in the District afore
said on Little River, waters of Savannah River bounded by lands of
Philip King, Robert McCraven, Wm. B. Herring, R. Derricott and others,
one third part of which decended to the said Jemima in fee, and the
balance to the said children above mentioned to be between them equally
divided, agreeably to the Act of Assembly as such case made and provided
That on the   day of   1818 your orator intermarried with the said
Jemima. That on the   day of   1819 the said Jamima departed this life
leaving an infant child the only fruit of her marriage with your orator.
That the said infant shortly after the death of his mother also died,
leaving no brother or sister of the whole blood. In consequence of the
premises aforesaid your orator became entitled under the Act of distribution of this State, to one third part of land to which the said Jer
Jemima late wife of your orator, was entitled in the tract above mention
oned, and the infant having died without brothers or sisters of the
whole blood, he also on his death became entitled as father and next of
kin, to the part to which he was entitled in the interest of his mother
in the tract of land above mentioned.

     Your orator further sheweth unto your honors, that on his intermarrage with the said Jemima as aforesaid, he took pleaded his case and protection the said Thomas L. Jeremiah E. and John L. Moore the children of the said Jemima by her former marriage, and maintained and educated them, from thence until sometime after the death of their mother which was about one year after her intermarriage with your orator, and he claims for the boarding cloathing &c of each one of the said children the sum of seventy five dollars pr year.

In tender consideration whereof, and for as much as the said minors are incapable of consenting to a partition of the said land, and a settlement of the said demand against them for their maintainance except under the direction of this honorable Court. To the end there fore that the said Thomas L. Jeremiah E. and John L. Moore may true, direct and perfect answer make to all matters and things aforesaid, and that a Writ of Partition may issue from this Court directed to certain Commissioners therein named requiring them to partition and divide the premises above mentioned, amongdthg parties aforesaid agreeable to the shares to which they are respectively entitled. And that the said Thomas L. Jeremiah E. John L. may be compeled to account with goud orator for their maintenance during the period above mentioned, and that your orator may have such other and further relief in the premises as from the circumstances of the case to your honors shall seem meet.

May it please your Honors to grant unto your orator your writ of Subpoena to be directed to the defendants requiring them on a certain day & under a certain penalty to appear in this Court to answer the premises aforesaid, and to stand to and abide by such order & decree in the premises as to your honors seem agreeable to Equity & good conscience.

And your orator will ever pray &c.

McComb & McCraven
Compt. Solr.

Filed June 10, 1820.

. . . .

ESTATE OF SAMUEL SCOTT PACK. 3356
BILL FOR ACCOUNT
CLERK OF COURTS OFFICE, ABBEVILLE, S.C.

The State of South Carolina
Abbeville District)
To the Honorable the Chancellors of the said State.
Humbly complaining sheweth unto your Honors your orator John A. S. Martin, that your orator while an infant became entitled to a large estate real & personal under the will of his grandfather Samuel Scott late of Edgefield District in the state aforesaid, by deed of gift from his father Charles Martin late of Edgefield District. That the said estate by reason of his tender years of your orator was comitted originally to the management of the said Charles Martin as guardian who entered into bond for the faithful discharge of his trust to the Commissioner in Equity for Edgefield District with Thomas P. Martin of Abbeville District as his surety. That the said Charles Martin having much wasted the estate of your orator, died in the state of Mississippi about the year 1810. Then the said Thomas P. Martin about the year 1811 opened unofficially the management of said estate, receiving large sums

of money for the rent of the lands & the hire of the negroes & other
services of profit until February term 1814 when he was regurlarly
appointed by the Honorable Court of Equity for Abbeville District guardian of the person & estate of your orator. That the said Thomas P.
Martin continued to act as guardian of your orator until his death in
182 (note by P.Y. no other number given.) That the actings of said
Thomas P. Martin as Guardian of your orator were very loose & irregular
in as much as he neglected to make regular annual returns, & in such
returns as he did make, omitted to charge himself with large sums of
money he had received & discharged himself for illeegal & improper dis-
bursements, but that by his own showing the said guardian at the time
of his death was indebted to your orator in the sum of (Note by P.Y.
no .amount was mentioned). That the said Thomas P. Martin shortly before
his death duly executed his last will & thereby appointed his son John
C. Martin Executor thereof who assumed upon himself the entire burthern
of the execution thereof. That upon the death of said Thomas P. Martin
your orator was not of full age & until his matyrity the said John C
Martin without proper authority managed his estate. That all the estate
of your orator with the rents issues & profits thereof, had passed into
the hands of the said John C Martin who has obstinately? refused upon
the frequent friendly applications of your orator, to come to any fair
settlement & account of your orators estate in his hands. That your
orator can have relief only in this Honorable Court. Where fore may ir
please your Honors to grant to your orator your writ of subpoena and
respendendum directed to the said John C. Martin requiring him to appear
in your Honorable Court to answer on his corporal oath the several
matters herein charged as fully as if herein you set down by way of
Interrogation. And then your honors would compel the said the said
(note by P.Y. written twice) John C. Martin to come to a full & equit
able account & settlement on your orators estate, & be ordered to pass
& deliver to your orator whatever shall be found due upon such account-
ing & that your Honors would grant such other & further relief as to
your Honors shall seem meet & equitable.

Filed 2nd Feby. 1830.

F. H. Wardlaw
Comp. Solr.

....

ESTATE OF EDWARD PRINCE SR.   PACK. 3357
BILL FOR INJUNCTION
CLERK OF COURTS OFFICE, ABBEVILLE, S.C.

South Carolina
Abbeville District) To the Honorable Henry Wm. Desaussure, Theodow
Gaillard, Thomas Waites?, William D. James and Waddy Thompson Judges
of the Court of Equity in the said State.
     Humbly Complaining, Your Orators and Oratrices, Robert F. Black and
(no name given here,P.Y.) his wife, Hudson Prince and (no name given
here, P.Y. his wife, and Edward Prince Jun. of the District of Abbeville
and State of South Carolina, respectfully Shew unto your honors. That on
the   day of   in the year of our Lord one thousand eight hundred and   , the late Edward Prince Senior made and duly executed
his last Will & Testament, by which after Specific legacies to sundry
persons, he devised and bequeathed to his wife Lucy Prince, all the

remainder of his property both real and personal, for her maintenance
and support during her life, and after her death he directed it to be
divided between your Orators & Oratrices Robert F. Black   and
his wife, Hudson Prince and   his wife and Edward Prince Junr,
Joseph Prince and his four grand children   Clark. That
afterwards sometime the said Edward Prince Senr. departed this life ,
leaving the said last Will and Testament in full force and unrevoked.

Your Orators&& Oratrices further Shew unto your honors that after
payment of the debts due by the Testator at the time of his death, and
the Specified legacies mentioned in the said Will, the remainder of his
estate was delivered by the Executors into the possession of the said
Lucy Prince who was entitled to the use thereof during her life as a
bove mentioned. That the said property consists of a considerable
real estate, twelve or thirteen negroes, a large stock of horses, Cows,
hogs &c. plantation tools and other planting Stock, together with
household furniture, and other property, amounting in the whole to the
value of twenty thousand Dollars or some other large sum of money, in
the possession and enjoyment of whichthe amount for life has remained
ever since.

Your Orators and Oratrices further Complaining shew unto your
honors that the said Lucy Prince being extremely old and infirm, and
from her weakness both of mind and body, easily imposed upon by crafty
and disguissing persons, has been induced to place the whole of the a
bove mentioned large property, under the direction of her son Joseph
Prince, a profligate? and disipated man, who is wantonly and intentionally wasting and destroying the said estate, and has already done
so to a very large amount, by the presumption of the said Lucy Prince
the tenant for life. That the said Joseph Prince has by the permission
of his mother disposed of a considerable partof the stock belonging
the estate and converted the money to his own use, as well as all the
proceeds of the Fortune to the value of two thousand Dollars pr. year,
and that he continues to mark the stock in his own mark and exercises
other acts of ownership over it, and even boasts that he will waste
and destroy the whole of this large property, in order to prevent your
Orators and Oratrices from dividing any advantage therefrom after the
death of the tenant for life.

And your Orators and Oratrices further shew unto your honors that
they have frequently both by themselves and others applied to the said
Lucy Prince in a friendly manner and requested her to take the property
from under the direction of the said Joseph Prince, and to prevent the
utter distruction of the estate, which would be the uncertainable consequence of its continuing under his controll. But with those reason
able requests the said Lucy Prince hath presumptiously refused to
comply. Sometimes pretending not to believe the great waste which was
making of the property, of which from her extreme debility and weak
ness she could know but little, and at other times refusing to listen
to the complaints which were made to her concerning the waste.

All which actings and doings are contrary to Equity and good Conscience, and tend to the manifest injury of your orators and oratrices in the premises.

In tender consideration whereof and for as much as your orators and oratrices are are (written twice,P.Y.) remediless in the premises except by the aid and assistance of this honorable Court where matters of this nature are properly cognizable and relievable.

To the end therefore that the said Lucy may be compeled upon her oath, to, true, direct and perfect answer make to all and Singular the matters aforesaid, and that as fully and particularly as if it was here again repeated, and interrogated. And that the said Lucy Prince may be enjoined from wasting & destroying the said estate farthe r than is necessary for her comfortable support, or permiting it to be so wasted and destroyed, and that your orators and oratrices may have such other & farther relief in the premises as to your honors shall seem meet.

May it please your honors to grant to your orators & oratrices your writ of Subpoena to be directed to the said Lucy Prince thereby commanding her at a certain day and underna certain penalty therein to be inserted, personally to be and appear before your honors in this honorable Court, then and there to answer the premises, and to stand to and abide by such Order and Decree therein as to your honors shall seem agreeable to Equity & good conseience.
And your Orators & Oratrices will ever pray &c.
McComb & McCraven
Filed 18th February 1820.   Compts. Solr.

. . . .

ESTATE OF JOHN WOOLDRIDGE   PACK. 3358
BILL FOR PARTITION
CLERK OF COURTS OFFICE, ABBEVILLE, S.C.

State of South Carolina
Abbeville District) To the Honorable the Court of Equity of the said State.
Humbly complaining, then unto your honors, your orators and orat- rixes James Harris & Frances his wife, which said Frances is the daug- hter of John Wooldridge deceased, Matilda Wooldridge, Lucy Wooldridge, Nancy Wooldridge, Susannah Wooldridge, Sally Wooldridge & Harriet Wooldridge, daughters of the said John Wooldridge, infants under the age of twenty one years by their guardian James Harris, William Wool- dridge, Thompson Allen & Betsy his wife which said William & Betsy are children of the said John Wooldridge decd. & infants under twenty one years of age, by their guardian Alexander Hunter. That the said John Wooldridge their father being seized & possessed at the time of his death of considerable real & personal Estate departed this life Intes- tate on the   day of   January in the year of our Lord one thous- and eight hundred & seventeen, leaving your orators & oratrixes & Patsey Wooldridge his widow & relict as his only heirs & distributees ; at law. Your Orators & oratrixes further shew unto your honors that on

the   day of   in the year of our Lord one thousand eight hundred
& seventeen, Thomas Wooldridge obtained letters of administration on
the personal estate of the said John Wooldridge from the ordinary of
Abbeville District & by virtue thereof the said Thomas possessed him
self of all the personal Estate of his intestate of great value viz.
fifteen thousand dollars or other large sum & hath sold or disposed
of the same & raised great sums of money thereby to two third parts or
shares where of your orators & oratrixes are entitle as aforesaid,&
your orators & oratrixes further shew unto your honors,that Gibson
Wooldridge the father of the said John Wooldridge & grand father of
your orators & oratrixes being seized & possesed of a considerable real
& personal Estate duly made & published his last will & testament in
writing bearing date on or about the 24th day of October in the year
of our Lord one thousand eight hundred & sixteen & thereby directing
his Estate to be sold & the money arising therefrom to be divided
according to the statute of distributions, & of his said will, he did
recommend & appoint his two sons the aforesaid John Wooldridge & Thoma
s Wooldridge the executors. And your orators & oratrixes further shew
unto your Honors that the said Gibson Wooldridge very shortly there
after departed this life, without altering or revoking his said will,
a copy whereof is herewith filed & marked exhibit A. And upon his said
death the said Thomas Wooldridge qualified under the said will before
the Ordinary of Abbeville District and took upon himself the Burthern
and execution thereof and by virtue thereof possessed himself of all
the Estate of the said Gibson Wooldridge to the amount of twenty thous
and dollars or other large sums & hath sold the same & received large
sums of money therefor, and your orators and oratrixes further shew un
to your Honors that the said Gibson Wooldridge left at his death en
titled to portions or shares under his said will the said John Wooldridge, Thomas Wooldridge & Robert Wooldridge. And your Orators & oratrixes further shew unto your Honors that the said John Wooldridge
died before he had received any part of the Estate of his said father
to which he was entitled under the will by reason whereof your orators
& oratrixes have become entitled to such portion or share together with
their mother the said Patsey Wooldridge. Your orators & oratrixes furth
er shew unto your Honors that the said John Wooldridge at the time of
his death was seized & possessed of a tract of land containing five
hundred and thirty six acres, more or less situate in Abbeville District
& lying on Savannah river, & bounded on the said River & lands of
Zachariah (no name here,P.Y.) Wm. Tucker & Ethel Tucker & also a
number of negroes about 8 at this time, to which said land & negroes
your orators & oratrixes are entitled to partition and division and to
receive & have two third parts thereof to be equally divided between
them. Your Orators & Oratrixes further shew unto your Honors that they
have ofben applied to the said Thomas Wooldridge in a friendly manner
to give them an accoubt of the personal Estate of the said John Wool-
ridge and of the Estate of the said Gibson Wooldridge & to make division & partition of the said negroes belonging to the Estate of the said
John Wooldridge & that he might pay over to them, what might appear due
to them from the said Estates & divide the said negroes & in like manner
they have often applied to the said Patsey Wooldridge & requested her
to join & concur with your orators & oratrixes in the necessary & prop-

er acts for making a fair & proper partition to the said land between
& among her the said Patsey & your orators & oratrixes, according to
the act of Assembly in such case made & provided, with which reason
able requests your orators and oratrixes well hoped that they would
have complied as in justice and Equity they ought to have done. But
now as it is it may if please your Honors, the said Thomas refuses to
give an account of the said Estates & to pay over to your orators &
oratrixes what may be justly due them & to make a division of the
said negroes & the said Patsey also refuses to join & concur with your
orators & oratrixes & doings of the said Thomas & Patsey an contrary
to Justice & Equity. In tender consideration whereof and for as much
as matters of this that are only relievable in a Court of Equity. To
the end therefore that the said Thomas and Patsey may respectively
true full and perfect answer make.

    And your orators & oratrixes will ever pray &c.

Filed 21 Nov. 1822.   Noble & Wardlaw
                                        Compt. Solr.

....

ESTATE OF NIMROD CHILES   PACK. 3359
BILL FOR PARTITION
CLERK OF COURTS OFFICE, ABBEVILLE, S.C.

The State of South Carolina
Abbeville District)   In Equity.
To the Honorable the associate Judges of the Court of Equity of the
said State.
    Humbly complaining your orator and oratrix John Presley and Ferr
by his wife and Reubin Golding & Susana his wife, William Stewart and
Eliza his wife, shew unto honors that Nimrod Chiles late of Abbeville
District deceased, was at the time of his death seized and possessed
of a considerable estate both real and personal, of which property
the said Nimrod Chiles made a disposition in his last will and testament a copy which is herewith filed. Your orators shew unto honors
that they have each of them intermarried, that is to say the said
Presley with Ferreby Chiles, the said Rhubin Golding with Lurana,
(note by P.Y. in one way the name looked like Lurana & another way
looked like Susana) Chiles, the said William Stewart with Eliza Chiles
all of them the daughters of the said Nimrod Chiles. Your orators and
oratrixes further shew unto your Honors that Nimrod Chiles the young
est of the children of the said Nimrod Chiles deceased will attain
the age of fifteen years on or about the   day of May next at which
time the division of the estate of the said Nimrod Chiles deceased is
directed to be made in and by his last will and testament. Your orators
and oratrixes further shew unto your Honors that Lucinda Chiles the
other daughter of Nimrod Chiles deceased has intermarried with one
Lewis Ball, who as your orators and oratrixes are informed have conveyed to Archey Mayson the Executor of the estate of the said Nimrod
Chiles deceased all their right, claim & title to their distributive

share of the said estate. Your orators and oratrixes further shew unto
your honors that some of the personal property of the said Nimrod
Chiles liable to distribution among his legatees is in the possession
of the said Archey Mayson one of the Executors of the said Nimrod
Chiles deceased. Your orators and oratrixes being desirous that the
division of the estate of the said Nimrod Chiles should be effected
pray that a writ of partition may issue to be directed to certain persons therein named to partition and divide the estate of the said
Nimrod Chiles among those interested or to recommend what would be
most conduced? to the interest of the parties therein concerned, that
the said Archey Mayson may be directed to surrender what property he
may have in his possession liable to distribution and also to dis-
cover to the Court what claim if any he may have to the distributees
share of the said estate. May it therefore please your honors to grant
to your orators and oratrixes your writ of subpoena to be directed to
the said Archey Mayson & Nimrod Chiles to appear in his honorable
Court and answer to the premises and to compel them to abide, by the
decree of this Honorable Court touching the premises.

                                              Mayson
Filed 14th Feb. 1820.   Comp. Sol.

WILL OF NIMROD CHILES.

In the name of God Amen. I Nimrod Chiles of South Carolina Abbeville
District and of sound and perfect mind and memory blessed be God do
this seventh day of may in the year of our Lord one thousand eight
hundred & five make and publish this my last Will and Testament in
manner and form following viz. first I leave my present Wife Elizabeth
Chiles during her natural life or widowhood provided she shall pay all
my just debts, bring up clothe and educate all my children while under
cover, for which I leave her in full possession of all my property
after my debts are paid and as long as she remains a widdow and no
charge is to be made against any of my Children when they receive
their portions for cloathing & Schooling as I deem my property more
than Sufficient for that purpose secondly and should my Wife marry
again in that case I give unto her during her natural life Coveture
only a part of my plantation or tract of land whereon I live to Start
from James Maysons dec.d line begain fineens? on the upper side and
run from thence up my spring branch a direct line untill it strikes
Walter Chiles land nearly South but the branch is to be the guide also
one third of personal estate but at her death both personal & real
estate is to be equally divided among my children herein after named
my allow any of them the privilege of settling on any of my land on
the east side of the above mentioned line as the West side is the part
allotted for my beloved Wife also the use of any part of my present
estate that they claim just & fair, but whenever my youngest child
my said wife may bear to me be fifteen years of age or at the death of
my beloved wife in either case the whole of my property lent to my
Children to be return and equally divided among them who may be alive
at that time and should any of my children marry before a division
takes place and dies leaving lawful issue such issue to share equally
as if there parents ware living but should they marry & die without

without issue than the property to be divided amongst my remaining
children (thirdly) Should I die with this present illness or previous
to my debts being paid and the crop then growing should be insufficient
to pay my debts tis my desire that part of my Stock of Cattle & hogs
be sold which eaver my Executor may think most proper for the advantage of my children to discharge the same (fourthly) my present children
are as follows Leoraney? — Levendey Elizabeth & Ferreby Childs and
should any be born nine months after my deth and be a girl to share
equally with the rest and should it prove to be a son tis my will and
desire that he shall have a tract of Land to contain three hundred
acres laid of ad joining that allotted to my beloved wife Walter
Childs & Mr Halls land as my beloved wife Elizabeth Childs will be
appointed as my Executrix in a future clause of my will when ever she
does mary I revoke and sett aside that part wherein I name her my
executor should such an event take place but if my beloved wife remains
a Widdow untill my youngest child be fifteen years of age I bequeath
unto her during her lifetime the same part of my Estate as if she was
to marry, the land left my Heir should it be a Son (word not plain) be
that much over and above his proportionable part of my estate also it
is my desire that my Executors take and return part in the management
of my Estate as I deem an Executrix insufficient by herself (eighthly)
I make and ordain this my last will and Testament and appoint my be
loved Wife during her widdowhood my Executrix Together with my beloved
friends Walter Chiles & Archey Mayson my Executors to carry this my
last will & Testament into execution. In witness whereof I the said
Nimrod Chiles have to this my last will and Testament set my hand &
Seal the day & year above written.
Signed Sealed & delivered published & declared
by the said Nimrod Chiles the Testator as & for his
last will & Testament in the presence of us who
were present at the signing and sealing thereof.
John C. Mayson
Robert Cox   Nimrod Chiles (L.S.)
John Chiles

Will proven April 10, 1819.

LEWIS BALL TO ARCHEY MAYSON.
State of South Carolina
Abbeville District) Know all men by these presents that I Lewis Ball
of the State of Georgia & County of Jasper in Consideration of the sum
of two hundred dollars to me paid by Archey Mayson of the State & District aforesaid have granted bargained sold and released and by these
presents do grant bargain sell and release unto the said Archey Mayson
all my undivided part of a Tract of Land formerly the property of Nimrod Chiles de.dleft by his will to be divided to his four Daughters
when his youngest child arives at the age of fifteen one of which
dughters I have married the said lands lye adjoining lands belonging to
Samuel Wardleworth Archey Mayson Joseph Hill and others in the State
and district aforesaid lying on a branch of Saluda River Together with
all & Singular the rights members hereditaments and appurtainances to
the said premises belonging or in any wise incident or appertaining

which I may have acquired by said marriage To have & to hold all and
Singular the premises before mentioned unto the said Archey Mayson
his heirs and assigns forever -- and I doe hereby bind my self & Each
& eavers of my Heirs Executors and administrators to warrant and for
ever defend all & Singular the said premises unto the Said Archey
Mayson his heirs & assigns against my self my wife and my heirs and
against eavery other person lawfully Claiming or to Claim the same or
any part thereof In Witness Whereof I have hereunto set my hand and
Seal this fourth day of October in the year of our lord one thousand
eight hundred & Eighteen & in the forty third year of the Americian
Independence
Signed Sealed & Delivered
in the presents of us   Lewis W. Ball   (SEAL)
Beaufort T. Watts
John P. Watts

....

ESTATE OF ROBERT S. PATTERSON   PACK. 3360
BILL FOR PARTITION
CLERK OF COURTS OFFICE, ABBEVILLE, S.C.

The State of South Carolina
Abbeville District) In Equity.
To the Honorable the Chancellors of the said State.
    Humbly Complaining shew unto your Honors your oratrix Mary D.
Patterson as follows.
    Robert S. Patterson late of the District & state aforesaid died
intestate leaving as his only heirs & distributees a widow your orat-
rix & two infant children to wit James Napoleon Patterson and Robert
Lewis or Sims? (note by P.Y. this name was to dim to make out ol early)
Patterson. Soon after the death of the said Robert S. Patterson his
son Robert died, then being an infant of very tender years. Wade S.
Cothran has been appointed the guardian of the estates of the other
son James Napoleon Patterson by this Honorable Court.

    At the time of the death of the said Robert S. Patterson he was
seized & possessed of a considerable estate real & personal. The real
estate consisting of one tract of land situate lying & being in the
state and district aforesaid on Bever dam creek waters of Hard labor
creek containing nine hundred & fifty acres more or less being the
tract of land which was allotted to the said Robert S. Patterson
under proceedings in this court to partition & divide the real estate
devised by Robert Smyth Senior to the children of Nancy Patterson of
whom Robert S. was one, whereon the said Robert S. lately resided,
bounded by lands of Josiah C. Patterson Jno. Lipscomb   Bulow
& others.

    Administration of the personal estate was committed to Josiah C.
Patterson who has sold all the personal estate and as your oratrix be
lieves paid the debts due by the said estate. The land now remains

subject to partition between your oratrix & her infant son James
Napolean Patterson.

In tender consideration whereof & for as much as your oratrix can
have adequate relief only by the aid of this Honorable Court.

And your orator will ever pray &c.

Filed June 14, 1836.

Wardlaw & Perrin
Compts. Sols.

(Note by P.Y. On another paper the name Lewis was correct.)

. . . .

ESTATE OF MRS. FRANCES HERRON   PACK. 3361
BILL FOR RELIEF
CLERK OF COURTS OFFICE, ABBEVILLE, S.C.

The State of South Carolina
Abbeville District)   In Equity.
To the Honorable the Chancellors of the said State.
        Humbly complaining shew unto your Honors your orator William
Campbell of the District and State aforesaid, that about the first
day of March in the year of our Lord one thousand Eight Hundred &
forty six Mrs. Frances Heron, John T. Heron and Mary T. Heron all
then of Abbeville District Confessed a Judgement to your orator for
the sum of (92.50) with interest thereon from the first day of January 1843, on a promissory note which they were owing to your orator,
& on the 5th day of March 1846, your orator lodged his Fiei Facices
in the Sherrifs office of said Disrict for the said sum above confessed together with fifteen Dollars twelve (15.12½ cash of the same
suit. That afterwards about the   day of   in the year 1846 & be
fore the payment of any part oof said Judgment & Execution, the
said Mrs. Frances Heron one of the said Defts, in said Exxoution departed this life intestate and administration of her estate has been
granted to George A. Miller of Abbeville District, who has possessed
himself of the effects and estate of said intestate but which your
orator is informed, believes and charges is very small, and not more
than sufficient to pay the costs of administration & the expenses
of her last illness, that John T. Heron and Mary T. Heron have left
the state and now reside beyond the limits of the same & that they
departed without paying the said demand of your orator or any part
thereof, and without leaving behind any property except that here in
after named, and which your orator is advised can be applied to the
satisfaction of his Executions aforesaid only by the interposition and
aid of this Honorable Court.

        That by the will of Thomas Heron decd. late of said district &
state, the husband of the said Frances Heron, and the father of the
said John T. & Mary Heron cectain property was bequeathed to the said

Frances his widow for & during the term of her natural life, and
after her death to his children, two of whom are the said John T.
Heron and Mary T. Heron. That after the death of the said Frances, as
aforesaid, to wit, about the   day of   in the year of our Lord
one thousand Eight Hundred and forty six, administration with the
will annexxd of thx said Thomas : Heron was also granted to the said
George A. Miller who has taken possession of said estate in remainder,
and by virtue of an order from the Court of Ordinary of Abbeville District has sold the same, the proceeds of said sale, your oratrix is
informed amounted to the sum of one thousand & Seventy nine dollars,
which after satisfying the debts, if any there be, of the said Thomas,
belong equally to the children of said Thomas as legatees in remainder under his will, subject to advances made to them by his widow in
her lifetime as by the said will she was authorized to do. The said
Thomas left five children, all of whom are alive. except one who has
left children surviving him. That the said Judgement & Execution of
your orator nor any part thereof, has not been paid either by the
said Frances before her death, nor by her administrator since, nor by
the said John T. Heron and Mary T. Heron or either of them before or
since their removal from the state, and your orator is advised that
the legacy in the hands of the said George A. Miller administrator
with the will annexxd of said Thomas Heron demands (word torn, P.Y.)
to the said John T. Heron & Mary T. Heron the surviving & absent defendants in said Exxcution is liable to the payment of his demands
and should be applied in satisfaction thereof, and that he has applied
to the said Geo. A. Miller & in a friendly manner requested him to
pay to your orator his demand as aforesaid out of the legacies in his
hands belonging to the said John T. and Mary T. Herron, but the said
George A. combining and confederateing with the said John T. and Mary
T. Heron & continuing how to wrong and injure your orator in the premises, refuses to comply with your orators reasonable request. All
of which actings doings & refusals are contrary to Equity & good
conscience & tend to the manifest wrong & injury of your orator.

    And your orator will ever pray &c.

                                        B.Y. Martin
Filed 15th Nov. 1847.   Comp. Sol.

            ... .

            ESTATE OF JOHN F. YARBROUGH PACK. 3362
            BILL FOR PARTITION
            CLERK OF COURTS OFFICE, ABBEVILLE, S.C.

The State of South Carolina
Abbeville District) In Equity.
To the Honorable Henry W Desassure and William Harper Chancellors
of the said State.

    Humbly complaining sheweth unto your Honors, your orator John W.
Yarbrough of the district and State aforesaid. That John F. Yarbrough

late of the District and State aforesaid, departed this life on the
fifteenth day of December one thousand eight hundred and twenty two
intestate, seized and possessed at the time of his death of a considerable real estate, situate lying and being in the District of Abbeville and State aforesaid containing in what is here called the
"Home Tract" four hundred and one acres more or less and composed of
several contiguous and adjoining tracts, and bounded by lands of D.
Pressly, John Laird Alexander Martin and Jesse Raigins and all comprehended in two plats of Resurvey made by John Cochran Deputy
Surveyor Dated 19th August 1817 and 8th March 1817, which plats
plainly describe the tracts boundings & buttings of the said tract of
four hundred and one acres as aforesaid, and containing in what is
here called "the Mountain Tract" four hundred acres more or less,
which tract was purchased at Sheriffs Sale in the lifetime of the
intestate, and titles executed to him by Alexander C. Hamilton then
Sheriff of Abbeville District in which titles the said tract of land
is represented to be bounded by lands of John Brownlee Robert
O Margy and others, and which two tracts make in the whole Eight hundred and one acres of which the intestate was seized and possessed,
at the time of his death. That the said John F. Yarbrough left as his
only heirs and Distributees the following persons namely Sarah Yarbrough his widow John W Yarbrough (your orator) Harriet C Yarbrough
now Harriet C Burley wife of John Fred.k Burley, Richard S. Yarbrough, James M. Yarbrough and Marcella E Yarbrough his children, three
of whom are minors without guardians viz Richard S. Yarbrough &
James M Yarbrough are minors over the age of fourteen years and Marcella E Yarbrough is a minor under the age of twelve years. That
the aforesaid real estate is now subject to division and partition
between Sarah Yarbrough the widow aforesaid, and John W Yarbrough
your orator Harriet C Yarbrough now the wife of John F. Burley,
Richard S Yarbrough, James M Yarbrough and Marcella E Yarbrough
children aforesaid who are all entitled to their distributive share
of the real estate aforesaid agreeably to the act of assembly of the
state passed abolishing the rights of premogeniture? and giving an
equal distribution of the real estate of intestates. Your orator
further shews unto your Honors that he is desirous that partition
should be allotted to him and his heirs forever in Severalty as in
justice and equity it ought to be done.

And your orator shall ever pray &c.

Filed April 7th 1830.

Thos. P. Spierin
Compts. Solr.

. . . .

ESTATE OF SAMUEL AGNEW   PACK. 3363
BILL FOR PARTITION
CLERK OF COURTS OFFICE, ABBEVILLE, S.C.

The State of South Carolina
Abbeville District) In Equity.
To the Honorable the Chancellors of the said State.

Humbly complaining sheweth unto your Honors your oratrix Malinda
Agnew as follows. Your oratrix is the widow of Samuel Agnew late of
the District aforesaid, now deceased, who died about the twentieth
day of July 1844 intestate, leaving nine children, to wit, Enoch
Agnew, Elizabeth Pressly the wife of Ebenezer E. Pressly, James W.
Agnew, Samuel Agnew, William Agnew, Joseph Agnew over the age of
twenty one years, and Washington Agnew, Alfred Agnew and Melinda Jane
Agnew under the age of twenty one years, who with your oratrix are
his only heirs and distributees.

At the time of his death the said Samuel Agnew was seized and possessed of a considerable quantity of land in seperate bodies or tracts
consisting of the following to wit. 1st. The Home Tract, whereon the
said Samuel Agnew died, lying on waters of Long Cane Creek, containing four hundred acres more or less, and bounded by lands belonging
to James Agnew Senr. Thomas Hawthorn and others. 2nd. The Mill Tract
containing about three hundred and seventy acres more or less, also
lying on waters of Long Cane Creek, and bounded by lands of Toliver
Johnson, James Blain and others. 3rd. The Andrew Agnew tract, also
lying also on Long Cane creek, containing about two hundred and
seventy acres more or less, and bounded by lands of James Agnew,
Enoch Agnew and Thomas Hawthorn.

Administration of the estate of the said Samuel Agnew has been
granted to Enoch Agnew and James W. Agnew, and your oratrix has heard
and believes that they have assets in their hands, arising from the
personal property largely and all the debts that can come against
the estate, so that now the land is subject to partition between
your oratrix and the nine children aforesaid and your oratrix is now
desirous of having partition made of the said lands, and her share in
severality assigned to her.

And your oratrix will ever pray &c.

Filed 29th May 1845.

Perrin & McGowan
Comps. Sol.

. . . .

ESTATE OF JACOB MARTIN PACK. 3364
BILL FOR PARTITION FOR SLAVES
CLERK OF COURTS OFFICE, ABBEVILLE, S.C.

The State of South Carolina
Abbeville District) To the Honorable the Chancellors of the said
State.
    Humbly complaining sheweth unto your Honors, your Orator Willie
B. Martin of the State and District aforesaid as follows. That on the
twenty eighth day of December in the year of our Lord one thousand
eight hundred and thirty Six, Jacob Martin of the Said State and District by a Deed of Gift (a copy of which is herewith filed marked A.
and to which reference is prayed) gave to Nancy Martin, the mother of

your orator, for and during her natural life or widowhood, the following named slaves and their increase, to wit, Linn?, Ephraim, Betsy, Jenny and Molley and at the death or marriage of the said Nancy Martin the said Slaves and their increase to the children of his Brother George W. Martin equally to be divided between the said children. That in the Spring or Summer of eighteen hundred and forty two, the tenant for life, Nancy Martin died, and your orator together with his Brothers and Sisters, to wit. Martha who intermarried in eighteen hundred and thirty with Milton Chiles, Rosanna E.A. who in eighteen hundred and thirty two intermarried with James Haddon, and Indianna who in eighteen hundred and forty two, and after the death of the tenant for life, intermarried with Thomas A. Benning, and John B. Martin who is a minor became entitled in remainder to the said slaves and their increase. Your orator to one fifth part and his brother and sisters to the remaining four fifths. The increase of the said slaves since the date of the gift are Hannah, Fanny, Amanda, Lety and Simpson. The said slaves are now on the premises where the tenant for life died and in the possession of Franklin Branch Executor of the tenant for life who as your orator is informed makes no claim on said slaves except of their works untill the ground crop is gathered.

    And your orator shall ever pray &c.

                                    J.H. Wilson

Filed 27th Sept. 1842.   Comp. Sol.

On one paper America R. E. Haddon was mentioned as wife of James H. Haddon.

DEED OF GIFT.

Know all men by these presents that I Jacob Martin of Abbeville District and State of South Carolina in consideration of the Love good will and natural affection which I have and do bear for and towards the children of my deceased brother George W. Martin and his widow Mrs. Nancy Martin I have given and granted and by these presents I do freely give unto the said Mrs. Nancy Martin for and during the term of her natural life or widowhood the following named negroes, to wit, Linn?, Ephraim, Betsy Jenny & Molly and their increase and future issue (the children they now have or may have here after) also I give to her as aforesaid all the plantation tools, household & kitchen furniture on the premises on which she at present resides after the decease or the marriage of the said Nancy Martin I do give the above negroes and their increase to the children of my brother Geo W Martin Equally share and share alike & allso the household and kitchen furniture & plantation tools to the said children as above mentioned. To have and to hold all and each and every of the above mentioned negroes, goods & chattels unto the said Nancy Martin for and during her natural life or widowhood, and after her decease or marriage unto the children of my deceased Brother Equally share and share alike, their heirs and assigns forever. And I do hereby bind myself my heirs executors and administrators to warrant and forever all and singular the goods and chattels above mentioned unto the sd.

Nancy Martin during her natural life or widowhood, and after to the
children Equally their heirs and assigns from myself my heirs Executors and administrators and from all persons whomsoever lawfully
claiming or to claim the same or any part thereof. Witness my hand
and seal this 28th day of December in the year of our Lord one thousand Eight hundred & thirty six
Signed Sealed and Delivered
in the Presence of   Jacob Martin   (L.S.)
Jeremiah T Gibert?
A. Hunter

. . . .

ESTATE OF JAMES McCULLOCH PACK. 3365
BILL TO ACCOUNT
CLERK OF COURTS OFFICE, ABBEVILLE, S.C.

The State of South Carolina
Abbeville District)   In Equity.
To the Honorable the Judges of the Court of Equity of the state
aforesaid.

  Humbly complaining your orator Alexander Sample shews unto your
honors that in the Fall Term of the year of our lord one thousand
eight hundred and eighteen he obtained a judgement in the Court of
Common Pleas of Abbeville District against William McCulloch &
John McCulloch Administrator of James McCulloch deceased for the sum
of sixty five dollars upon which judgment your orator has a Feri
Facias issued in the usual Form against the said William McCulloch
and John McCulloch upon which a return of Nulla Bona has been made
by the sheriff of Abbeville District all of which appears of Record
in the respective offices of the Clerkand sheriff of the District
aforesaid. Your orator farther shews unto your Honors that since the
obtaining the judgment aforesaid the said William and John McCulloch
have removed out of the limits of this state, so that no other pro-
cess against them can be had.

  Your orator further shews unto your Honors that at the time
of obtaining letters of Administration on the estate of the said
James McCulloch deceased, the said William McCulloch and John McCulloch entered into a bond with Taliaferro Livingston Esquire ordinary
of the District aforesaid for the time being in which said Bond John
E Norris and Andrew Gilespie were bound as sureties, which said
bond was conditioned in the usual Form.

  For as much as the said Administrators have committed or Devas-
tavit of the estate of said James McCulloch deceased,& for as much as
the said Judgment obtained against them with the cost therein has
not been paid & satisfied – and also for as much as your orator is
without complete and adequate remidy except by the aid of this Honor
able Court, your orator prays that the said William McCulloch and
James McCulloch and the said John E Norris and Andrew Giliespie
may decreed to come to a fair and just account for his judgment

aforsaid with his cost thereon incurred.

And your orator will ever pray &c.

Filed 26th Dec. 1820.

Mayson
Compt. Solr.

....

ESTATE OF MARGARET CALDWELL   PACK. 3366
BILL FOR PARTITION
CLERK OF COURTS OFFICE, ABBEVILLE, S.C.

The State of South Carolina
Abbeville District)   To the Honorable Henry W Desaussure Theodore
Gaillard, Thomas Waters, Waddy Thompson & W.D. James Judges of the
Court of Equity of the said state.

Humbly complaining sheweth unto your Honors your orator and
oratrix Alexander Stewart and Peggy his wife. That   Caldwell
(note by P.Y. no first name given) late of Abbeville District in the
the State aforsaid some time since departed this life intestate,
seized and possessed at the time of his death of a considerable real
estate consisting of a tract of land Situate in the district afore
said containing three hundred thirty acres more or less and bounded
by lands of Samuel Young Joel Lipscomb & others on Quarter Creek
waters of Saluda River and leaving at the time of his death your
oratrix Peggy his widow & relict and who has since intermarried with
your orator Alexander Stewart and the following children William
Caldwell, Alexander Caldwell, Sibby Wilson wife of Drury Wilson
_ formerly Sibby Caldwell, Elizabeth Caldwell, Margaret Caldwell,
Edmond Caldwell James Caldwell John Caldwell Polly Caldwell Jesse
Caldwell Belinda Caldwell and Sarah Caldwell his only heirs and distributees. Your orator and oratrix further shew unto your Honors
that your oratrix Peggy is entitled to one third part of said land
in fee according to the act of the general assembly in such made &
provided and the remaining two thirds are subject to division among
the children aforesaid. Your orator and oratrix further shew unto
your Honors that they have often applied to the said William, Alexander, Drury and Sibby his wife, Elizabeth Margaret, Edmond James
John Polly Jesse Belinda & Sarah and requests them to join with your
oratrix in the necessary acts & proceedings to make such partition,
with which reasonable request your orator & oratrix well hoped they
would have complied as they ought to have done.

And your orator & oratrix shall ever pray &c.

Filed 14 Feby. 1820.

Noble
Compt. Solr.

....

State of Georgia
County of Cass

Know all men by these presents that I James H Linn of the County of
Cass and State aforesaid have constituted made and appointed, and by
these presents do make constitute, and appoint John W Weems of the
same County and State my true and lawful Attorney for me and in my
name and Stead and for my use to ask demand sue for recover and receive all such Sums of Money debts accounts deus or other demands
whatsoever that are or shall be due owing payable or belonging to
me or detained from me, and which may be in the hands of the Commissioner of Equity of Abbeville District in the State of South Carolina, or in the hands power or possession of any other person coming
or resulting to me from the Estates of J F Hill and Eliza M Hill,
formerly Linn, or in any other manner Giving and granting to my said
Attorney by these presents full and whole power Strength and authority in and about the premises, to have use and take all lawful means
and ways in my name for the recovery thereof, and upon the the receipt of any such dues demands sum or sums of money aforesaid acquitt-
ances or other Sufficient discharges for me and in my name to make
seal and deliver, and generally all and Every other act and acts
thing and things necessary to be done in and about the premises for
me and in my name to do and Execute and perform as fully largely and
amply to all intents and purposes, as I might or could do if I were
personally present, or if the matter required more special authority
than herein given, and attornies one or more under him for the purpose aforesaid to make and and Constitute, and the same at pleasure
to revoke, ratifying affirming and holding for firm and Effect ual
all and whatsoever my said Attorney Shall or may lawfully do in and
about the premises by virtue hereof.

In witness whereof I have Set my hand and seal dated at Cassville
the thirty first day of August in the year of our Lord one thousand
Eight hundred and fifty nine and in the the Eighty third year of the
Sovereignty and Independence of the United States of America.
Signed Sealed and acknowledged
in presence of us
Thos. M. Compton?   James H. Linn
John A Crawford
Not Pub Cass County Ga

Georgia
Cass County) I hereby Certify that John H. (note by P.Y. written H
here instead of A) Crawford, whose genuine Signature appears to the
foregoing Power of attorney as ex official witness and before whom the
same was Executed is and was at the time an acting Notary Public in
and for Said County duly authorized and Sworn as Provided for by the
Statute in such case made and provided and as such is entitled to full
faith and credit in his official acts.

Given under my hand and Seal of office at Cassville Ga. This 31st
day of August 1859.

John T. Millain? (check on this
name, was'nt postive)
Clerk Inf. Court Cass Co

Georgia
Cass County) I, Maddison McMurry acting Judge of the Inferior Court
for Cass County Georgia do hereby Certify That John T. (check this
name in Ga, to be sure,P.Y.) whose genuine Signature appears to the
foregoing Certificate is the acting Clerk of said Inferior Court of
Cass County Georgia. That his Signature Hereto is genuine. That said
certificate is in due form of Law, and that said Court is a court of
Record &c.
    Witness my hand and official Signature Done at Cassville Ga.
Aug. 31st 1859.

M. McMurry J.I.C.

................,,,,

WILLIAM H. CALHOUN TO J.H. WILSON PACK. 501
POWER OF ATTORNEY
CLERK OF COURTS OFFICE, ABBEVILLE, S.C.

Know all men by these presents that I William H. Calhoun of the
County of Pontotoc and State of Mississippi have made constituted
and appointed and by these presents do make constitute and appoint
Jno H Willson of Abbville Dist my true and lawful attorney for me
and in my name and for my use, to ask demand sue for recover and receive all such sum or sums of money debts goods wares and other demands whatsoever which are or shall be due owing payable and belong
ing to me by any manner or means whatsoever Especially or Selling
of certain land known as the Cabbin lands, in Abbeville Dst So Ca
giving and granting unto my said attorney by these presents full
power and authority in and about the premises to have use and take
all lawful means in my name for the purposes aforesaid and upon the
receipt of any such debts dues or sums of money acquitences or other
sufficient discharges for me and in my name to make and give and
generally to do all other acts and things in the law whatsoever
needful and nesesery to be done in and about the premises for me and
in my name to do Execute and perform as fully largely and amply to
all intents and purposes as I myself might or could do if personly
present, and attornies one or more under him for the purpose afore
said to make and constitute and again to revoke at pleasure, Hereby
ratifying allowing and holding for firm and effectual all and whatso
ever my said attorney shall lawfully do in and about the premises
aforesaid by virtue hereof in witness whereof I have hereunto set my
hand and seal the 20 day of January 1858.
Witness
F. or T? Richman   W Henry Calhoun
Samuel C. Gill

....

State of Florida
Sumter County) Know all men by these presents that I, S H Clay of
aforesaid State & County, do hereby nominate, constitute and appoint
my mother viz Elizabeth Clay of the District of Abbeville and State
of South Carolina my true and lawful attorney, irrevocable in my
name or otherwise, for the following purpose to wit to collect ask
for, demand if necessary sue for, receive and recover the sum of
Five hundred and Fifty Seven dollars and Eight Cents the said sum
being now in the possession of and due from W.H. Parker, Commissioner in Equity for the District of Abbeville State of South Carolina, the said sum being due the undersigned as an inheritance from
his Fathers Estate, giving and granting unto my said attorney full
power & authority to do and perform every act, deed, and thing,
requiste and necessary in the premises, as fully, to all intents
and purposes, as I might or could if this assignment or Power of
attorney had not been made, with full power of substitution & Re-
vocation, hereby ratifying and confirming all that my said attorney
or her substitute may lawfully do or cause to be done, in the premises by virtue hereof. In witness whereof I have hereunto set my
hand and seal, this the Eigth day of october one thousand eight
hundred and sixty (1860)
Signed, sealed and delivered in the
Post office at Sumterville Fla   S.H. Clay (L.S.)
in presence of
W.C. Williams
J.E. Williams

State of Florida
Sumter County) I B O Grenade? Clerk of the Circuit Court for
Sumter County state of Florida do hereby certify that S H Clay per-
sonally appeared before me and acknowledged his signature to the
above instrument of writing granting a Power of Attorney to his
Mother Elizabeth Clay for the purposes therein mentioned as witness
my hand and the seal of the Circuit Court on this the Eighth
October A D 1860
                    Benj. O. Grenade?   Clerk of the Court
                                        Sumter County Fla.

. . . .

CAROLINE & ROBERT MEEK TO JAS. F. MABRY
POWER OF ATTORNEY   PACK. 501
CLERK OF COURTS OFFICE, ABBEVILLE, S.C.

The State of Mississippi
Holmes County) Know all menby these presents that we, Robert D.
Meek, and Caroline C. Meek, (formerly Caroline C. Mabry, but now
intermarried with the said Robert D Meek) of the county and state

aforesaid having full confidence in James F Mabry of Abbeville
District in the State of South Carolina, do hereby appoint and constitute him my attorney in fact to ask, demand and receive of and
from the commissioner in equity of Abbeville District and state of
South Carolina aforesaid, whatever sum or sums of money that may be
in his hands belonging to or due to the said Caroline C Meek as
heir at law of Reubin L. Mabry late of said Abbeville district and
state of South Carolina, deceased, arising from the sale of lands or
real estate of said deceased by said commissioner, and upon whose
receipt thereof by or payment thereof to my said attorney we do
hereby authorize and empower him a release or discharge for the
same to make execute and deliver. And we do hereby ratify confirm
and allow whatsoever our said attorney shall lawfully do in the
premises.

In witness whereof we do hereunto set our hand and affix our
seals the 25th day of August A.D. 1857.

Caroline C Meek (SEAL)
R D Meek   (SEAL)

State of Mississippi
Holmes County) Personally came before me Richmond J. Brown Judge
of Probate of said County - Robert D Meeks and Caroline C Meeks
his wife who severallyacknowledged that they signed sealed and de
livered the foregoing Deed or Power of attorney as their voluntary
act and deed on the day and year therein mentioned for the purposes
therein specified and the said Caroline C. wife of the said Robert
D. Meeks having been examined by me privately, separate and apart
from her said husband, acknowledged that she signed sealed and delivered the same as her voluntary act and deed freely without any
fears threats or compulsion on the part of her said husband.

Given under my hand and private seal (there being no seal of
office this 25th August 1857.

Richmond J. Brown (SEAL)

The State of Mississippi
Holmes County) I Armstead G Otes? Clerk of the Probate Court in &
for said County do hereby certify that Richmond J Brown whose name
is signed to the foregoing certificate of acknowledgement is now &
was at the time of signing the same Judge of the Probate Court in &
for said County duly elected qualified & commissioned according to
law & that all his official acts an & should be entitled to full
faith & credit.

Given under my hand & seal of office at Livington? the 3d day
of Sept 1857.

A G Otes? Clk

....

South Carolina
Ninety Six District) To the Honorable the Judges of the Court of
Equity of the said State.

      Humbly complaining, sheweth unto your Honors. your Orator
John Brackenridge of the District & State aforesaid (Weaver) that
your orator, on the fourteenth day of November in the year of our
Lord one thousand seven hundred & ninety five, being indebted by
Bond to a certain Mathew Donaldson of the District & State afore
said (word not plain, P.Y.) deceased, in the sum of three hundred & forty pounds lawful sterling money of the State aforesaid
equal to Fourteen hundred & forty six dollars, eighty six cents
apiece Conditioned for the payment of one hundred & twenty eight
dollars & forty three cents in three annual instalments to wit,
the sum of two hundred & forty two dollars eighty one cents on
or before the twenty third day of april one thousand seven hundred and ninety six two hundred & forty two dollarseighty one
cents on or before the twenty third day of april in the year of
our Lord one thousand seven hundred snd ninety seven, and the
remaining one third on or before the twenty third day of April
one thousand seven hundred and ninety eight that for the better
securing the payment thereof your orator did agree to mortgage
to the said Mathew Donaldson the property herein after mentioned.
And accordingly your orator did execute to the said Mathew Donaldson a Bargain and sale, bearing date on or about the fourteenth
day of November one thousand seven hundred and ninety five, and
by the said Bargain & sale, your orator for and in consideration
of the debt aforesaid of seven hundred and twenty eight dollars
& forty three cents, and the better securing the payment thereof
to the said Mathew Donaldson his certain attorney , heirs, executors administrators or assigns on or before the terms of payment above specified, bargained and sold Mathew Donaldson, a
quantity of very valuable personal property, consisting of negroes Horses cattle House hold & kitchen & other valuable (word)
to a very considerable amount, subject to a proviso or condition,
that if your orator his heirs Executors or administrators should
well and truly pay or cause to be paid unto the said Mathew
Donaldson or to his certain attorney heirs, executors, administrators or assigns the full and just sum of one hundred and seventy pounds equal to seven hundred & twenty eight dollars & forty
three cents, at the times mentioned in the obligation aforesaid
that then the deed of Bargain and sale should be void and of none
effect. And in case default should be made on the payment of the
said sum of seven hundred & twenty eight dollars, forty three
cents according to the true intent and meaning of the said condition, that then & in that case it shall and may be lawful for
the said Mathew Donaldson from time to time & at all times there
after, quietly to enter into any or all the nesuages lands or
tenements of your orator and to take possession of the bargained
premises together with the issue and increases of the property
therein mentioned from thence forth snd forever, or the same to

sell and dispose of at his will and pleasure, returning the over
plus if any should happen to be after paying the said sum of
seven hundred and twenty eight dollars forty three cents unto the
said John Brackenridge his heirs executors or administrators. All
which will more fully & satisfactorily appear on refering to a
paper herewith exhibited marked A. And your orator further states
to your Honors, that immediately on the execution of the mortgage
aforesaid, to wit on the same day, the said Mathew Donaldson in
tered upon and took possession of the mortgaged property aforesai'
d and continued to use occupy and ebjoy the same together with
the increase and profits thereof from the day of the date of the
conveyance aforesaid up to the time of his death. That shortly
after the execution of the mortgage aforesaid, and before the
first instalment aforesaid became due, the said Mathew Donaldson
took upon himself to sell and dispose of a considerable part of
the mortgaged property and continued at his will and pleasure to
sell and dispose of the said property from thence up to the time
of the last payment becoming due, at which time, the property
thus disposed of, taking into (word) the times when, and the
prices thereof, if they can be correctly ascertained would have
been quite sufficient to have discharged the obligation aforesaid
& have completed with the true intent and meaning of the mortgage
aforesaid. But not with standing the premises aforesaid the said
Mathew Donaldson continued to sell dispose of and use occupy and
enjoy the said mortgaged property until his death, ref using to
come to any account with your orator respecting the premises, or
to deliver over to your orator the mortgage aforesaid and what
remained of the said mortgaged premises aforesaid, and thus con-
tinually refused up to the time of his death. Your orator begs
leave further to state to your Honors that during the period a
bove mentioned your orator (word) unto the said Mathew Donaldson
many very important personal services, labor and industry, to a
considerable value, which your orator hopes will be taken into
consideration as forming just debts and set offs against the
different instalments due on your orators bond. Your orator further states, that sometime in the latter part of the month of
November in the year of our Lord one thousand eight hundred and
two the said Mathew Donaldson departed this life, leaving a last
will and testament duly executed, thereby having constituted and
appointed John Bowie Seni:or, James Wardlaw Esquire, George Bowie
Esquire & Andrew Bowie the executors of his said will. (Note by
P.Y. The rest on this paper was'nt so important.)

State of South Carolina

This Indenture made the Second day of August, Anno donini One
thousand Seven hundred and Ninety one and in the Sixteenth year
of Anerician Independence Between John Langerds, of the State of
South Carolina and County of Abbeville of the one part and Will-
ian Burton of the said State and county of part of the other
part. Witnesseth that the said John Langerds for and in Consider
ation of the sun of Twelve pounds Sterling Money of south caroli
na to hin in hand paid by the said William Burton hath granted
bargained and sold, alienated Released and Confirmed and by
these presents doth bargain and sell alien Release and Confirm
unto the said William Burton, In his actual possession (word
torn) by Virtue of a bargain and sale tohin thereof nade by In
denture bearing date thereof next (several words torn) after
Stated in transfering uses into possession and to his heirs and
assigns forever all that parcel or tract of land Containing one
hundred and nine acres, Situate lying and being in Abbeville
County on Johnsons Creek of Savannah River it being part of a
tract of Seven hundred and thirty three acres of land granted
unto Henry Watkins, By his excellency Charles pinckney Esqr.
Governor connander in cheif & over of the said State at Charles
ton, the sixth day of April Anno Donini one thousand seven hundred and eighty three in the thirteenth year of Anerician Independence, and Recorded in the Secretarys in Grant Book Z.Z.Z.Z.?
(page 277) buttind and bounding and having such shapes forn and
Marks as are delineated and described in plat hereunto Innexed,
Together with all and Singular the houses, out houses, Fences,
trees, woods water, water Courses, way the paths passages,
(several words torn) and any thing Whatsoever thereunto be
longing or in any wise appertaining and the Reversions & Rever
sions, Renainder and Renainders, Rents Issues and profits there
of to have and to hold the said parcel or tract of Land contain
ing one hundred and nine Acres nore or less of land and all and
Singular other the premises hereby granted and Released unto the
said William Burton his heirs and assigns to his and their only
proper use and behoof forever fron hin the said John Langerds
his heirs and assigns, and the said John Langerds for hinself his
heirs Executors, Administrators doth hereby covenant and grant
to and with hin the said William Burton, his heirs and assigns
that the said John Langerds his heirs, Executors and Adninistrat
ors shall & will at all tines hereafter warrant and defend the
said tract of land fron the said the said (written twice,P.Y.)
John Langerds, his his heirs and assigns for ever. In witness
whereof the said parties to these presents their hands and seals
have hereunto set on the day and year first above written.
Signed Sealed and Delivered
In the presents of   John Langerds
Adan Crain Jones Jur.
Nathaniel Barnes
Henry Tallow or Fallaw?

Recorded March 28, 1792.
(To whom it may concern. The following deed was badly torn
and faded, I copied it to the best of my ability.P.Y.)

....

ESTATE OF JOHN McKELLAR SR. PACK. 3368
BILL FOR ACCOUNT
CLERK OF COURTS OFFICE, ABBEVILLE, S.C.

State of South Carolina
Abbeville District) To the Honourable the Chancellors of said
State.

Humbly complaining sheweth unto your Honors your orators
John W. McKellar , and William B. McKellar for themselves,and
James D. McKellar, by his guardian the said John W. McKellar.
That some time in the year A.D. eighteen hundred and seventeen
John McKellar Senior the grand uncle of Complainants died in
testate, seized and possessed at the time of his death of a
large real estate, principally lying in the District, and the
adjoining District of Edgefield. At the time of his death the
said John McKellar Senior left various relations in this State
and in Scotland. But as your orators were the nearest of kin
who could inherit real estate according to the laws of this
State they were decreed? to be legally intitled to all the
real estate of the said John McKellar Senior, in accordance
with the prayer of a Bill filed in this Honourable Court on
the seventh day of December A.D. eighteen hundred and eight
een, by the father of Complainants, John McKellar Junior, as
their guardian. Before the time when the said Decree of this
court in the matters above refered to had been made, the said
John McKellar Junior died intestate, and as your orators were
then of very tender years, all of whom were under the age of
fourteen years Charles C. Mayson Esquire then of the District
and State aforesaid was appointed their guardian in accordance
with his petition to this Honourable Court at June Term A.D.
eighteen hundred and nineteen, and immediately thereafter proceeded to discharge the duties of guardian under the authority
of this Court. Soon after the time when this Honourable Court
had decreed the lands in question to belong to Complainants,
and after the time when the said Charles C. Mayson had been
constituted the guardian of your orators, and had commenced
the discharge of his duties, as such, to wit, at June Term A.D.
eighteen hundred and twenty, the said Charles C. Mayson as
guardian of Complainants petitioned the court to sell certain
lands for the purpose of **defraying** the expenses of the procedi
ngs in Equity aforesaid, & for the purpose of supporting Complainants, and an order was granted to that effect. But complainants have not been able to ascertain what lands were sold
under this order, nor the amount for which they were sold.
Complainants further show unto your Honours that the said

Charles C. Mayson, as their guardian, did further petition this
Honourable Court, at June Term eighteen hundred and twenty to
have all the real estate to which Complainants were entitled
sold, and subsequently at February term eighteen hundred and
twenty two the whole of the land was ordered to be sold by the
Commissioner in Equity for this District, except two tracts up
on extended credits, with interest from the date of sale, to
be taken with securities for the payment of the purchase money,
all which will appear by reference to records of this Honourable
Court, Complainants further affirm that they are well informed,
that the whole amount of the real estate to which they are en
titled from the grand uncle aforesaid, amounted to considerably
more than seven thousand acres, and was worth at the time when
the order for sale was obtained between twenty and thirty thou
sand dollars. Complainants further shew, that under the two
orders refered to, nearly all the land in question has been
disposed of either by their guardian, the said Charles C. Mayson
or by the Commissioner in Equity, for which large sums have
been received, and upon the principle sums due large amounts of
interest have accrued. Yet Complainants have received but a
small portion of what they conceive themselves to be entitled
to and although the Bonds under the order of court were taken
in the name of the Commissioners, yet complainats are informed
and believe that they have all been handed over to the said
Charles C. Mayson, and the moneys arising therefrom have been
received by him. Complainants further shew, that although the
said Charles C. Mayson has made regular returns, as the guard
ian of all expenditures on account of Complainants, yet he has
not been equally diligent in making a return of all the receipt
s in favour of Complainants. This conduct Complainants can but
regard as injurious. (Note by P.Y. The rest of this paper
was'nt so important. So did not copy to save space.)

And your orators will ever pray &c.

Lesly & Cothran
Filed January 1, 1836.   Compts. Sols.
One paper dated Dec. 30, 1835 mentioned that Cas. Mayson was
residing out of the state.

. . . .

ESTATE OF MICHAEL MEYER PACK. 3369
BILL FOR DISCOVERY
CLERK OF COURTS OFFICE, ABBEVILLE, S.C.

State of South Carolina
Southern Circuit) In Equity.
To the Honorable Hugh Rutledge, William Marshal and William D.
James Judges of the Court of Equity.

Humbly complaining sheweth unto your Honors your Orators
John Prior of the District of Edgefield in the State aforesaid
and Sally his wife. That Michael Meyer in the District of Edge

field in the State aforesaid, being seized and possessed of a
very considerable real and personal estate, did on or about the
twenty third day of November in the year of our Lord one thous-
and seven hundred and eighty four duly made and publish his
last will and testament in writing and thereby among other
things devised and bequeathed as follows. I give and bequeath
the remainder of the above mentioned tract of land being one
hundred and thirty acres lying at the west end known by the
name of Mother Pegs place to the three Children of my Son
Leonard deceased named Grace, Sally and Leonard to be rented
out to the best advantage by my Executors, for the mentainance
of the said Children till such time that my Grand Son shall be
of age, and if he should die before he is of age, till such
time that my Grand Daughter Sally shall be of age or married,
and my will is that my sons David or Jonathan, or either of
them, pay to the above named three children the sum of one hun
dreddred and fifty pounds Sterling, and then the above mention
ed land by me left for the maintenance of the above named Chil
dren ', be the property of my sons David and Jonathan, or
either of them, or him, and their or his heirs forever, but if
my two sons nor either of them should choose to pay the above
mentioned Sum, then my will is that the said land should be
sold by my Executors and the money equally divided amongst the
Children that then may be alive, and my will is that if my two
sons David and Jonathan should agree for to sell their land
then in that case I desire that the part that I have left the
use of for the maintainance of my grand children above named
shall also be sold with their lands, and the money that it
fetches to be put out at interest, or young negroes to be bought out of it for the Childrens use, and that my sons David and
Jonathan pay each fifty pounds Sterling out of their, part of
the money of their land so sold to my two Daughters Elizabeth
and Catharine. Item I give and bequeath the remainder of my
Estate such as plantation tools household goods, and books, and
if any of the Negroes now in my possession should prove to be
my property, to my five Children to be equally divided amongst
them and the Children of Leonard deceased, and that the said
Testator did nominate and appoint his three sons John David and
Jonathan with Casper Nail Senior his Executors to his said last
will and Testament. That the said Testator died on or about the
day of   in the year of our Lord one thousand seven hund
red and   . That the said John, David and Jonathan and
Casper Nail Senior duly proved the said will in the Court of
Ordinary of Ninety six District and took upon them the and
execution thereof, and accordingly possessed themselves of all
the said Testators real and personal estate, goods chattles
and effects to a very large amount. That the said John Meyer,
Jonathan Meyer and Casper Nail Senior three of the above named
Executors are since dead, that John Meyers one of the said Exe
cutors leaving Mary Nancy and James his children and heirs, and
that administration of all and singular his goods and chattels
rights and credit was granted to Jesse Roundtree and that the
said Elizabeth died leaving Jonathan her heir and Executor as

your orators are informed and verily believe died intestate.
Jonathan Meyers another of the said Executors and Executor of
the said Elizabeth daughter of the said Testator, duly made
and Executed a last will and testament, and appointed Casper
Nail Junior, George Bender and David Meyers Executors thereof,
that Catharine Meyers a daughter of the said testator died
having duly made her will and left Michael?Wright and David
Meyers Executors thereof, and that Casper Nail Senior duly made
and executed a last will and appointed Casper Nail Junior Executor thereof. That Leonard Meyers son of Leonard and grand son
to the said Testator died intestate on or or about the   day
of   in the year of our Lord one thousand   whilst
young and before he arrived to the age of twenty one years.That
your orator and oratrix intermarried on or about the   day of
in the year of our Lord one thousand   . That your
oratrix is one of the daughters of Leonard Meyers Senior deceased and grand daughter to the said Testator mentioned in the
said Will, and that your orators purchased from Grace Meyers
daughter of the said Leonard Senior and Grand Daughter of the
said Testator all her right title and interest in and to the
personal estate goods and chattels(or her share and portion
thereof) to her left by the said Testator in his said will,she
the said Grace, at the time of the said purchase being legally
of age to dispose thereof. Your orators further complaining
shew unto your honors that the said Land by the said Testator
in his said Will, left for the use and mentainance of the said
Grand children was and now is very valuable, that it might have
been rented for a considerable sum yearly. That the said John,
David, Jonathan, and Casper Nail Senior, and since the death of
the said John Jonathan and Casper Senior, the said David, Geor
ge and Casper Junior, neglected to rent out the said land for
the use of the said Grand children, or to sell the said land
and put the purchase money out at interest, or to lay it out in
the purchase of young negroes, or in any other manner to dispose of
of the said land or the price thereof for the benefit mentain
ance and education of the said Grand children, as in his said
Will the said Testator directed should be done, and that they
have not nor hath either of them rendered any Account of the
personal estate of the said Testator, or made any division
thereof among the said Grand Children according to the true in
tent and meaning of the said Testator in his said Will express
ed. Your orator further complaining shew unto your orators that
since their intermarriage as aforesaid they have at various
times applied to the said David Meyer and to the said John
Jonathan and Casper in their lifetimes and since their death to
the said George and Casper Junior their Executors as aforesaid
requesting them to pay to your orators the rent or its value of
the said land, and the money due to them for the sale of the
said land in value thereof in young negroes, and to satisfy
your orators for their interest in the said land under the said
will of the said Testator. (Note by P.Y. The rest on this paper
wasnt so important, P.Y.)   Filed 24th Oct. 1805.

WILL OF MICHAEL MEYER OF BEACH ISLAND.

In the name of god amen, I Micheal Meyer of the State of South
Carolina Ninety Six District, planter being weak in Body but
perfect in Mind and Memory, thanks be to god for it, but knowing
that it is appointed for all Men once to Die and not knowing
how soon my Change may Come Do therefore make and ordain this
my last will and Testament hereby revoking and disanulling all
former wills made by me Principally and first of all, I Bequeath
my soul to god who Gave it in hopes of his gracious Exceptance
of the same in and throu the Merits and Mediation of our Lord
and Savious Jesus Christ — And my Body to be decently buried, —
and as to the worldly goods with which it had pleased god to
endow me after my just debts are paid I do bequeath in Manner
and form following. I give and bequeath to my son John the track
of Land I now live on — And which we three Brothers took up to
gether under one grant in the year one thousand seven hundred
and thirty Seven, Containing One Hundred and fifty acres more
or less for which track of Land we all three Brothers agreed
among ourselves not to sell nor to part with any of the said
Land except by Consent but the longest Liver should have all
for himself — and his Heirs for ever and that the said track of
Land is willed to me Mich.l Meyer and to my Heirs by Both of my
Brothers Leonard and Ulrick?in thare Last wills and Testaments
tharefore I give and Bequeath to the Above Mentioned son John
said track of Land to him and his heirs forever. Item I give
and Bequeath to my other two sons David and Jonathan each one
Hundred & thirty acres of Land part of a track of three Hundred
and Ninety Acres in Beach Island on Horse Shoe pond the said
Land to be laid out to them on the Est side of said Tract of
land the lines to be run North and south, and the one that has
the best tract in value for to make up the value in some other
property to the one that his tract is of lesser value and if
thay cant agree amongst themselves in setling the value of
Said land so devided, in that case they shall leve it to three
men to settle and what said men for that porpes chosen settles
it as they shall stand to, said Land then being to them and
their Heirs forever. Item I give and Bequeath the use of the
remainder of the above mentioned tract of land being one hundred
and thirty acres lieng at the West end known by Mother pegs
place, to the Three Children of my Son Leonard Deceased named
Grace Sally and Lenord to be rented out to the best advantage
by my Executor for the mentance of said Children, til such
time that my grand son shall be of age, and if he should Die be
fore he is of age til such time that my Grand Daughter Sally
shall be of age or maried and then my will is that my sons
David and Jonathan or Ither of them pay to the above named
three Children the sun of one hundred and fifty pound Sterling
and then the above mentioned Land by me left for the mentance
of the above mentioned Children be the property of my sons
David and Jonathan or to either of them that pays the above sun
of money to the said Children to them and there or his Heirs

forever, but if my Two sons nor either of them should chose for
to pay the above sum then my Will is that said Land should be
sold by my Executors and the money equally devided amongst the
Children that then may be alive and my Will is if my two sons
David and Jonathan should agree for to sel there Land then in
that case I desier that the part that I have left the use of
for the maintanence of my Grand Children above named shall all
so be sold with there Lands and the money that it fetches to be
put out at Interest or young negroes to be Bought out of it for
the Childrens use, and that my sons David and Jonathan pay each
fifty pounds Sterling out of there part of the money of these
Lands sold to my two Daughters Elizabeth and Catherine. Item I
give and bequeath to my two Daughters Elizabeth and Catherine
a tract of Land Joining Land laid out to John Jacob Sturzene-
grer containing two hundred acres more or less to be equally
devided between them as they may agree, and that my said Daughters may be made near equal with my sons there land not being
so valuable. I therefore bequeath to my Daughter Elizabeth one
Negro Boy named Jack and one Negro Wench named Filles, and to
my Daughter Catherine I bequeath one Negro Girl named Jenny and
one Negro fellow named Fortun, and I allso give to each of my
Daughters the choice of a Feather Bed and Furniture, and I give
my Stock of Cattle and Hoggs, to them both, and my two Horses,
to have And to hold the said property to them and thare Heirs
forever and my will is if either of my Daughters should die
single then the other to have the whole of the Land, and my
will is Also that my two Daughters as Long theay Remain Single
shall have the use of my House, garden, and yard, and as much
of the plantation as they can tend with the help of thare Negroes for thare Mantanence, but as soon as one is Marfied she
has no more Right to the House nor plantation. Item I give and
Bequeath the Remainder of my Estate such as plantation tools,
household, goods and Books, and if any the Negroes now in my
posession should prove to be my property, to my five Children,
to be equally divided, amongst them and the Children of
Leonards Deceast.

And to prevent trouble and Expence my Desire is that thare
may be no appraisment nor sail of my Estate only in the Land that
I have pointed out, if it should be taught adviseable by my
Executors, but just to have the will proved and Recorded, so
that each may have And enjoy thare parts according to my true
intent and meaning. I nominate and appoint my three sons John
David & Jothn. with my friend Casper Nail Senr. My Executors to
this my last will and Testament Declareing it to be such not
with standing any former will or wills By me Made. In witness
whareof I have hereunto Set my hand and Seal this twenty third
Day of Novr. and in the year of our Lord one thousand seven
Hundred and eighty four.
Signed Sealed and Declared in the
presence of ous   Michael Meyer
John Clarke
John Savage
Zacariah Johnston

WILL OF JONATHAN MEYER.

In the name of God Amen
I Jonathan Meyer of Edgefield County State of South Carolina
do make and ordain this to be my Last Will and Testament in
manner and form following, Vizt. In the first place it is my
Will and desire that my Executors hereafter named do in confor-
nity to my Fathers Michael Meyers Will pay to the two Surviving
Children of my Brother Leonard Meyer, Grace & Sarah Meyer, one
hundred and fifty Pounds Sterling Money which sum was directed
by the Will of my Said Father to be paid to the said Leonard
Meyers Children when they should come of age, in lew of Land
left me by said Will of my Father on paying the Children of my
Said Brother Leonard Meyer one hundred and fifty Pounds Sterling
and my Executors are to take a general discharge and release for
all matters and things from the said Grace & Sarah Meyer, that
being done and they satisfied no accounts of my Estate for there
support and maintainance are to be brought against then but
should they be Dissatisfied and refuse to comply with the in
tention of this Will in that case my accounts for advances for
there support are to stand good against then. I give and Bequeath to my well beloved Daughter Betsey Meyer all my Lands
all my Negroes Stock of all kinds, household Furniture, Plant
ation Tools, Bonds, Notes, Book, Debts, dues, and demands and
all property whatsoever that I shall die possessed of, but if
she Should die before she attains the age of Twenty one years
or leave Issue before she attains the above age of Twenty one
years that is if she dies died (written twice,P.Y.) without
Children under one & twenty years, in that event of her deceas
before she is one & Twenty and without Children all my property
is to be divided in the following manner Vizt. In case of the
deceas of my Daughter Betsey before she is one & Twenty years
& without Issue I give and Bequeath to my Brother David Meyer
two thirds of all my Property both real & personal dureing his
Natural life and after her decease to be equally divided among
his Children I also give and Bequeath my said Brother David my
Riding horse and wearing apperell.
    I also give and Bequeath in case of the deceas of my **Dau**-
ghter Betsey aforesaid the remaining one third of my Real and
personal Estate to be equally divided among the Children of my
late Brother John Meyer & the Children of my late Brother
Leonard Meyer.
    It is my Will and desire that my Negroes shall not `hired
out but kept to work the land under the direction of my Executors untill my Daughter comes of age or is married & Should
there be occation of hiring any of then out that the negroes be
hired out at private sale by my Executors and it is my Will &
desire that my Cattle, Sheep and houshold & Kitchen Furniture
(except my best Bed and Furniture be kept for my Daughter) be
sold after my Decease. I nominate and appoint my Brother David
Meyer, Mr. George Bender Mr Casper Nail to be Executors of this
my last Will & Testament I also nominate and appoint said David
    Meyer George Bender and Casper Nail to be guardians to my

Daughter Betsey Meyer, untill she come of age or shall Marrey
but in case any or all the guardians should die or refuse to act
It is my Will & Desire and I postively injoin it that my Daught
er Betsey Meyer shall never have it in her power to chose any of
the name or family of James Gray of Savanah for a guardian in
witness whereof I have hereunto set my hand & seal this 10 day
of Apl. 1802
Signed Sealed and Delivered in presents of
Cradock Burnell
Wm. Shinholser   Jonan. Meyer (SEAL)
Daniel Hail Senr.

. . . .

ESTATE OF W.T. & LOUISA JONES PACK. 3370
CLERK OF COURTS OFFICE, ABBEVILLE, S.C.
BILL FOR ALIMONY

South Carolina
Abbeville District) To their Honors the Chancellors of the
said State.
     Humbly complaining show unto your Honors your oratrix Louisa
Jones who sues by her next friend Beaufort T. Watts. That on
or about the   day of December in the year of our Lord one
thousand Eight hundred and forty your oratrix intermarried with
Dr. W. T. Jones of the District and State aforesaid, and continued to live with him untill some time in November Eighteen
hundred and forty one during all which time she demeaned her
self towards the said William T. Jones as kind, affectionate
and obedient wife and in every respect performed and fulfilled
her duties as such so far as his unkind and cruel conduct to
wards her would permit her to do. That not with standing her
constant and affectionate attention to the said W.T. Jones and
her continued and unwearied Exertions to please him, he by a
series of of abusive and cruel treatment after .their inter
marriage made her life a constant service of tension? Your
oratrix further shows unto your Honors that shortly after their
intermarriage the said William T. Jones gave Evidences of his
dislike to, and want of affection for your oratrix which was
Exhibited by his avoiding so far as he could the society of
your oratrix and by coarse and offensive language and remarks
will calculated to mortify and wound the feelings of your
oratrix. He also permitted and as your oratrix has just grounds
to believe encouraged his children by a former wife, to treat
your oratrix with great rudness and to charge her with acts and
conduct of the most improper character, such as secretly taking
articles from the house that did not belong to her and convey
ing them to others. He also refused to permit your oratrix to
visit her friends and relations, not even allowing her to go to
see a Sister who resided in the neighborhood. He locked your
oratrix up in his house and deprived her of all society of her

friends saying that the company of her servants about the house
was good enough for her. That your oratrix submitted with pat-
ientfortitude to all this harsh and mortifying treatment untill
about the month of August 1841 when the said William T. Jones
forgetful of the obligations which he owed to your oratrix and
to himself as her husband resorted to violence, inflicting up
on your oratrix at one time a severe blow with his hand and
shortly afterwards without any reasonable provocation two
severe blows with a hickory. When your oratrix finding that
she could not live with him in safety, determined ro leave him,
and in November 1841 , his improper treatment still continuing
your oratrix left his house and has continued to live separate
from him ever since. Your oratrix further shows your Honors
that at the time of her intermarriage with the said William T.
Jones she owned Eight negroes to wit a girl named Emily a
negro woman named Fanney and her six children Tom, Hannah,
Deal?, Mary, Betsy and Jenny and other personal chattels all
of which property on her marriage went into the possession of
the said W.T. Jones, and Still remains in his possession &
the said William T. Jones is possessed of other large estate
and altho your oratrix has been driven by the persecution and
violence of the said Jones from his house and forced to seek
shelter and protection amongst her friends and relations, the
said Jones still retains possession of the property which in
justice belongs to your oratrix, and which should be surrend
ered to her and refuses to make any provision whatever for the
confortable support and maintenance of your oratrix, leaving
her to depend entirely upon ` the charity of others for the
means of subsistance.

    And your oratrix will ever pray &c.

                                  Young & Perrin
Filed 26 April 1843.   Compt. Sols.

. . . .

                       ESTATE OF MATHEW MAYS PACK. 3371
                       BILL FOR PARTITION
                       CLERK OF COURTS OFFICE, ABBEVILLE, S.C.

South Carolina
Abbeville District) In Equity.
To the Chancellors of the said State.
Humbly complaining sheweth unto your Honors your orators and
oratrixes Larkin Mays, Henry Mays, Stephen Whitley and Eliza-
beth his wife (formerly Elizabeth Mays), Thomas Rosamond and
Sarah his wife (formerly Sarah Mays) Elias Graham and Caroline
his wife (formerly Caroline Mays), as follows.

    Lucretia Mays, widow of Matthew Mays who died a few years
since, late of the District aforesaid, departed this life on
the   day of February in the year of our Lord one thousand
eight hundred and forty five, intestate, leaving as her next
of kin and distributees your orators and oratrices, Medy Mays

Jr. her son who is of age, and the following minor children,
Nancy Mays, Daniel Mays, Abney Mays, Jane Mays, Tolitha Mays
and Lucretia Mays. At her death, besides her personal estate,
Lucretia Mays was seized and possessed of a tract of land,which
she had lately purchased of one Benjamin Rosamond, containing
two hundred and fifty acres more or less, situate in and near
Mulberry creek waters of Saluda River in the District aforesaid,
and now bounded by lands of Col. Larkin Griffin, John Waters
Esqr. your orator Larkin Mays, the Misses Philips, William
Graham Senior, and of your orator Thomas Rosamond, and which
constituted her whole real estate.

Your orators and oratrices further show unto your Honors
that the said Medy Mays Jr. is administrator of the personal
estate of the said Lucretia Mays deceased, and will have abund-
ant assets in his hands therefrom, to pay the debts of the in
testate, and they desire that partition of the said tract of
land be made between and among the said distributees of the
said Lucretia Mays deceased.

                                        John Cunningham
Filed May 2, 1845.   Com. Sol.

. . . .

ESTATE OF HUGH MORROH   PACK. 3372
BILL FOR INJUNCTION
CLERK OF COURTS OFFICE, ABBEVILLE, S.C.

State of South Carolina
Abbeville District) To the Honorable the chancellors of said
State.

Humbly complaining Showeth unto your Honours your orators
Enoch Darmore and Sarah his wife, Johnson H. Sharp and Jane
Caroline his wife, Pinckney Jones and Eleanor his wife all of
Abbeville District and State aforesaid. That on the   day of
Hugh Morr oh departed this life having duly made and published
his last will and testament, whereby he bequeathed to Jane
Morroh his wife for ever during her natural life considerable
property both real and personal, and upon the death of the said
Jane Morroh directed that the said property should go to his
four daughters to wit, Sarah, Jane and Eleanor your oratrices,
and Mary Morroh to them and their heirs forever. The personal
property bequeathed to Jane Morroh, and at her death (word)
over to her daughters, consisten of some slaves to wit Hannah,
since dead, Linda, Lucretia, Drewson?, Charlotte, Lewis, Saml.
Harry or Solomon and Sarah, together with the Stock of horses,
cattle, sheep, hogs, household and kitchen furniture, plantation
tools, books, &c. all of which property was by the Executors
placed in the possession of the said Jane Morroh, The slaves are
all living except Hannah who died in 1842 of a disease contract
ed on Savannah river whilst in the possession of the said Jane
Morroh. Three of the surviving slaves, Saml Linda and Lucretia
have since the death of the testator been by the said Jane

Morroh placed in possession of her son David Morroh who resides
in a sickly part of the District on little river, the said
slaves were placed in his possession about one year ago at the
time that he went to housekeeping where they have ever since
remained, and as your orators believe, have been given by the
mother to her son. The said Jane Morroh at the same time gave
to her son David a gray mare which was part of the property be
queathed to her for life only. She has also given to her son
John D. Morroh a borough? part of the said bequest to her for
life. The said Jane Morroh owns no property as your orators be
lieve but that bequeathed to her by the testator for life. She
has accumulated nothing, and is not likely to do so from the in
come of her life estate, but spends the whole of the proceeds
and profits either in the maintanance of herself and family or
in bounties to her sons whose interests she seems disposed to
promote, regardless of those of her daughters. And your orators
being wrongly? apprehension that the property bequeathed to
them in remainder would be wasted or removed beyond the limits
of the state and their rights or remainder were thereby dis-
troyed or endangered and yet being unwilling to harrass or
disturb the tenant for life in the full possession and enjoy
ment of her life estate, called upon the said Jane Morroh and
requested her in a friendly manner to give to your orators some
security for the forthcoming of the said personal property, up
on the determination of her life estate, which she refused to
do, at the sametime threatening to sell or give away the property as she ought be disposed,

And your orators will ever pray &c.

J. H. Wilson
Comps. Sol.

Filed April 15, 1844.

LAST WILL AND TESTAMENT OF HUGH MORROH DECD.

South Carolina
Abbeville District. In the name of God, amen. I Hugh Morrah
of the State and District aforesaid being of sound and dispos-
ing mind and memory but weake in bodey and calling to mind the
uncertainty of life and being desirous to dispose of all such
worldly Estate as it has pleased God to bless me with do make
and ordain this my last will in the manner following (viz) I
desire that immediately after my death that my Land and other
property not otherwise disposed of be sold and all my just debt
s and funeral expenses be paid.

Item 1st. I will, bequeath and devise to my wife Jane Morrah
(viz) the home tract of land and stock of Horses cattle sheep
Hogs household and kitchen furniture plantation tools &c on the
home place on Long Cane Creek together with the following property (viz) Solomon Harry Hannah and her five children and
Sarah and all the Books with her name in them during her natural life and after her decease I give the same to my daughters
(viz) Sarah Jane and Elinor and Mary to them and their heirs
forever.

Item 2nd. I will and bequeath unto my son Robert the sum of

one thousand dollars.

Item 3rd. I will & bequeath unto my son John the sum of five dollars.

Item 4th. I will and bequeath unto my son Samuel two negro es named Sam and Carwick also I will and bequeath unto my said son Samuel, five hundred acres of Land being a part of my plantation on Savannah river this land I allow to be taken off the upper line and to contain the Land known by the Downey Tract.

Item 5th. I will and bequeath unto my son Samuel the sum of two thousand Dollars.

Item 6th. I will and bequeath unto my son David the sum of four thousand dollars the interest of said sum I allow to pay the Education of my said son David.

Item 7th. I will and bequeath unto my Daughter Jane two negroes (viz) Sylvia and Peggy also the sum of one thousand Dollars.

Item 8th. I will and bequeath unto my daughter Elenor three negroes (viz) Polly and her twochildren Jim & Louisa also the sum of one thousand Dollars.

Item 9th. I will & bequeath unto my daughter Mary two negroes (viz) Dick & Frances also the sum of one thousand dollars.

Item 10th. I will & bequeath unto my son George the sum of five thousand dollars.

Item 11th. I will & bequeath unto my daughter Sarah the sum of five thousand Dollars.

Item 12th. I will and bequeath unto my daughter Sarah (wife of John Richardson) a large bay mare (Called Doll) also the sum of one Hundred dollars.

Item 13th. After the foregoing bequests are fulfilled & should there be a balance of property remaining it is my desire and order that it should be given to my wife Jane Morrah.

Item 14th. I hereby nominate and appoint Patrick Noble , Aaron Lonax & my son Samuel Morrah Executors of this my last will and testament wholly revoking and disannulling any former wills & testaments, by me made and hereby ratifying and order ing this to be my last will and testament done this second day of February in the year of our Lord one thousand Eight hundred and thirty seven and in the sixty first year of amer- ican Independence . Signed Sealed Published and Declared in the presence of the testator.

William Hill   H. Morrah (LS)
Wesley C. Norwood
M? T. Stewart

• • • • , •

ESTATE OF McALISTER WILLIAMSON PACK. 3373
BILL FOR DELIVERY OF SLAVE
CLERK OF COURTS OFFICE, ABBEVILLE, S.C.

The State of South Carolina
Abbeville District) In Equity.
To the Honorable the Chancellors of the said State.

Humbly complaining sheweth unto your Honors, your orator
McAlister Williamson, a citizen of the State of Georgia, resi-
dent in the County of Jones as follows. In the month of February in the year of our Lord one thousand eight hundred and
thirty seven, John, the male slave of your orator, departed
his service and plantation in the State of Georgia, without his
knowledge and against his wishes, and the diligent search and
audacious? inquiry thought to your orator for a long time no
certain intelligence of his said slave. The utter fruitless of
all the efforts which your orator made to ascertain where his
said slave John was during his abscence, caused your orator
to act that he had been (word) (Note by P.Y. This paper was so
dim and writing was so bad I just could not make out the rest
of this paper.) Filed 23 Sept. 1842.

South Carolina
Abbeville District) Personally came before me McAllister
Williamson and made oath that three witnesses attended from
Georgia in his behalf in the case of McAllister Williamson vs.
Samuel Beard, to wit, Hosea Johnson from Jones County, Georgia,
one hundred and thirty five miles from Abbeville Court House,
Isaac Willingham Sr. and Isaac Willingham Jr. each living in
Lincoln County Ga. about thirty five miles from Abbeville Court
house. That these witnesses were duly subpoenaed, and proved
their Subpoena tickets before H A Jones Esq for the purpose of
taxing the same up. That said witnesses attended four days in
Abbeville District at Abbeville Court H use by virtue of the
said Subpoena tickets, and even duly sworn except the last who
material to said deponent, but was excused by the court . his
testimony was supposed unnescessary by the testimony being
fully given by him was (word) That the said five dollars for
the Commission sent in his behalf to Henry County Georgia, and
three dollars for the commission sent to Jones County Georgia.
Sworn to and subscribed this 17th July 1844
    before me
Thos. Thomson   McAlister Williamson
Magst. A.D.

BILL OF SALE.

Georgia
Fayette County) Know all men by these presents that I John C
Depositer of the State and County aforesaid for and in consider
ation of the sum of eight hundred dollars to him in hand paid
by Nelson Bullard of the county of Henry & State aforesaid the
receipt whereof I do hereby acknowledge have bargained and sold
and by these presents do bargain and sell unto the said Nelson
Bullard his heirs and assigns the following property, one negro
man by the name of Foot about 40 or 41 years old to have and to
hold the aforesaid Bargained property to him the said Nelson
Bullard his heirs and assigns forever and I the said John C.
Depositer for myself my heirs and assigns and administrators
all and singular the said bargained property unto the said

Nelson Bullard his heirs and assigns against myself and my
said Executors and administrators and all other persons what so
ever claiming will forever defend by these presents.

In witness whereof I have hereunto set my hand and seal this
15 March 1837 signed sealed and delivered in the presents of
Samuel Hustan   John C. Depositer (LS)

On another paper.

Allen E. Johnson sworn states, "I know the negro John when he
belonged to Henry M. Pope in Henry County Georgia. I do not
know how long he was in the possession of Williamson. I do not
know when he left the complainant possession. I first heard of
the negro John about the middle of the month of June in the
year eighteen hundred and forty two. I received the intelligen
ce of him from Nelson Bullard. I called at the Penitentiary of
this State and obtained from the principal keeper leave to to
converse with Nelson Bullard who is now a convict hoping to
obtain from him information about a horse that had been stolen
from me, and in the conversation I then had with Bullard he
told me about the negro John and stated to me that he carried
John from this state to South Carolina and sold him to a man
by the name of Samuel Beard. Bullard stated to me that he received the negro from James Henry of Henry County Georgia to
gether with a bill of sale made by a man by the name of Depositer or Foster (or some such name) and Samuel Houstan of
Fayette County Georgia to him (Bullard) and when he sold the
negro he made no bill of sale but delivered over to Beard the
one he got with the negro from James Henry.

Henry M. Pope sworn states," I know the slave John, I know him
from the time he was born in the year seventeen hundred and
ninety four until my agent Eli Strickland sold him to complain
ant in January eighteen hundred and thirty seven. I cannot say
how long he remained in complainants possession., nor can I say
of my own knowledge when the negro left complainant. I heard
of the negro being lurking in Henry County Georgia in February
1837. I received this information from Hezekiah Hudman and
William L. Stark who caught him while performing patrol duty
and believing him to be still my property they stated to me
that they whipt him and set him at liberty again. The next I
heard of him was in the year 1840. I was told by John M. Chap-
man of this county that the negro John was in South Carolina.
John belonged to Jesse Norman my grandfather when I first knew
him. At the sale of my grand fathers property after his death
I bought him and continued to own him until Eli Strickland my
agent sold him to complainant.

William Winbish, Charles D. Bostick and Bennett Bridges of
Jones County, Georgia were also witnesses.

. . . .

State of South Carolina
Abbeville District) In Equity. To the Honorable Henry W.
Desaussure and Job? Johnston Chancellors of the said State.

Humbly complaining sheweth unto your Honors, your orator
John Middleton Hamilton of the District and State aforesaid,
state, that he is one of the legal distributees of Alexander C
Hamilton his father decd. and entitled to a share of the estate
of which his father died seized and possessed of at his death,
and is desirous of obtaining by Partition his share of the real
estate of his decd. father. That his father Alexander C Hamilton departed this life on the twenty seventh day of February one
thousand eight hundred & thirty five, Intestate, and seized
and possessed of a considerable real estate, distributable to
his surviving legitimate children Viz Jane, who is now the wife
of Genl. John Bowie, John .. Hamilton your orator, Robert B.
Hamilton, Susan now the wife of Jas. S. Wilson, Rich.d And.w
Hamilton, Joseph Augustus Hamilton, Alexander Hamilton, Samuel
Shields Hamilton, Anna Augusta Hamilton and Harriet Eugenia
Davis Hamilton the six latter children being now minors under
the age of twenty one years viz. Rich.d And.w Hamilton, Joseph
A. Hamilton, Alexander Hamilton, Samuel S. Hamilton, Anna A.
Hamilton and Harriet E.D. Hamilton. Your orator further States
that the said real estate of which his father died seized and
possessed is situated lying and being in the District and State
aforesaid on the waters of Norris's Creek, a branch of Long
Cane Creek, contiguous to the Village of Abbeville, containing
five hundred & twenty six & three fourths acres and bounded by
lands belonging to the Estate Alexander Martin decd. Maj. James
Alston,   Kary, & William C. Black being the same land as
appears by Exhibits A & B herewith filed. That your orator is
desirous of having the whole of the said real estate Partitioned
conformably to the Act of the Legislature of this State in order
to obtain his share in severalty separate & apart to his own use
benefit & behoof forever.

And your orator shall ever pray &c.

Thomas Pierrey Spierin
Filed May 16, 1835.   Compts. Solr.

This land was about half a mile north of the Village of Abbe
ville. .. O e paper mentioned that in 1835 that Robert B.
Hamilton was residing out of the limits of the state..

. . . .

ESTATE OF JOHN HILL SR. PACK. 3375
BILL FOR ACCOUNT
CLERK OF COURTS OFFICE, ABBEVILLE, S.C.

The State of South Carolina
Abbeville District)   In Equity.
To the Honorable the Chancellors pf the said state.

Humbly complaining shew unto your Honors your orator Robert C.
Richey & oratrix Nancy his wife ,and your orator William C.
Hill as follows.

Many years ago John Hill Senior departed this life having
made his last will and testament. By his will the said John
Hill Senior gave to his wife Susannah the plantation whereon he
lived with all his movable property together with the following
negroes to wit, Sylla, Cessa with five boys, Lewis, Silas, John?
Willis & Wiley during her widowhood, but provided that if his
wife should marry again that then she should have Cessa, one
horse and saddle one bed & furniture and household and kitchen
furniture during her life, and at her death the same to be equa.;
lly divided amongst his children. And upon the termination of
the life estate he gave to his son Samuel the negroboy Lewis,
to his son William the negro boy Silas to his son John the neg
ro boy Job? to his son Joseph the negro boy Willis and to his
son Bluford the negro boy Wiley. The testator also directed
that the said slaves should remain in the hands of the executors until each of the Sons should Severally be married or come
to the age of twenty one years, and in case any one of the said
slaves should die before the said sons should be entitled to
receive thence that out of the increase of Sylla or Cessa the
defeciency be made up.

The said John Hill Senior at the time of his death left as
his only heirs & legatees, a widow Susannah and twelve children
to wit, Betgy who intermarried with David Hill and by him had
several children only two of whom are now living to wit Jane or
Jiacy? now the wife of James Dodson and Joyce now the wife of
Cogburn , she afterwards married Patrick Gemain? and
had one son Thomas, and then died. Nancy then and now the wife
of William Mays. Polly then and now the wife of Jesse Rainey.
Sally then and now the wife of David Vines. Susannah, who inter
married with Benjamin Rosamond now dead, leaving as her only
heirs and distributees her husband the said Benjamin Rosamond
and seven children to wit, James, Benjamin, Samuel, John, Thomas
William and Joseph. Fanny now the wife of Samuel Rosamond.
Samuel Hill now dead, who left as his only heirs and distributees a widow Elizabeth who has since intermarried with William
Hodges and two children, to wit, Nancy your oratrix who has
intermarried with your orator Robert C. Richey and Elvira who
has since died unmarried and quite young. Administration of
Samuel Hills estate was granted to William Darmore.

William Hill who attained the age of twenty one years,
married and then died leaving as his only heir and distributee
William C. Hill.

John Hill who died leaving a will of which mention is
hereafter made.

Joseph Hill, who died intestate, leaving as his only heirs
and distributees a widow Eliza now the wife of JohnGraham.
and three children Susan, Jane & Frances.

Bluford Hill who died in his minority and unmarried.

About the year 1824 John Hill Junior died after having made
his last will and testament, by which he bequeathed to his
mother during her life or widowhood the said slave Gabriel, or
Gabe? and upon her marriage or death to be sold and the proceeds to be divided between his brothers Samuel, Bluford and
Joseph and his sister Rebecca all the residue of his estate,
he gave to the three brothers and sister above named. He appointed Reuben Hodges, Samuel Hill and William Barmore Executors of his will of whom William Barmore was the acting execut-
or.

Most of the property given to Susannah Hill as aforesaid
soon after the death of John Hill Senior passed into her possession, and some of the negroes for a number of years were
hired out. About the year 1838 the negro Gabe or Gabriel was
hired to David Vines and Nelia Vines under a contract that he
should be returned at the end of the year, and delivered up to
the said Susannah Hill or her agent. But the said David Vines
and Nelia Vines having failed to return the said slave Gabe at
the end of the year, about the twenty fifth of february 1839
an action of trover was brought by the said Susannah Hill a
gainst the said David Vines & Nelia Vines to recover damages
for his commission and about the seventeenth of october a verdict was rendered in favour of the said Susannah Hill against
the said David & Nelia Vines to the amount of nine hundred and
eighty three dollars, which was the full value of the said
slave Gabe.

Susannah Hill died about 1842. (Copied the most important.
Filed June 21, 1845.

WILL OF JOHN HILL SENIOR.

In the name of God Amen. I John Hill of the State of Abbeville
being weak in body but of perfect mind and memory Thanks be to
God calling to mind the mortality of my Body, and knowing it
is appointed for all men once to die, do make and ordain this
this my Last will and Testament. That is to say I give and
commend my soul to Almighty God that gave it and my Body to be
in a decent manner -- and as Touching such wordly Estate where
with it hath pleased god to bless me in this life I give de
vise and dispose of in the following manner- first I give and
bequeath to my Beloved wife Susannah the plantation whereon I
now live with all my movable property Together with one Negro
Wench Named Sylla and one named Cissa with five boys, one named Lewis, one Silas one Gabl. one Willis and one named Wiley
for for and durcing the term of her widowhood Excepting as is
hereafter mentioned- and my will is that if my beloved wife
Should marry again She Shall have the above named negro Cissa,
one horse and Saddle, one bed and furniture, and house and
kitchen furniture during her life and then to be disposed of
with other property as will be hereafter mentioned and like
wise in case my wife marries an other husband, the plantation
whereon I now live Together with the five Negro Boys and the
Negro wench Sylla is to be rented or hired by my Executors to
the highest bidder yearly - for the for the suport and school

ing of any of my children that may not have grown up. and my
will is that my Son Samuel Shall have the Negro boy Named
Lewis -- that William Shall have Silas-- that John Shall have
Gab.l-- that Joseph shall have Willis, and that son Bluford
has Wiley.

Nevertheless the above five Negro Boys is to remain in the
hands of my Executors untill each of my above Named Sons are
Severally married, or of the age of Twenty one years, and in
case any of the above named negro Boys Should die before my
Sons are Entitled to receive them, my will is that out of the
increase of Sylla or Cissa the said deficiency Shall be made
up.

My will is that my Negroes named Ben -- Hannah, Mina and
Linda be sold by my Executors on a credit of Twelve months and
the amt arising therefrom to be Eaqualy devided between my
Daughters Betsey -- Nancey, Salley-- Susannah, Fanny -- and
Rebecca, or in case they would wish to keep the negroes in the
Family the Negroes is to be Valued by three Freeholders, and
any one of my Children wishing to take a Negro at the price so
put on, may have them by paying to my Executors the Ballance
Sd Negro may be over their part, at the Expireation of Twelve
months after delivery of said Negro, with Interest for Sd
Ballance from Sd delivery-- Nevertheless be it Remembered that
out of the price of Sd four Negroes my will is that my Daughter Polly be paid by my Executors the sum of Fifty Dollars and
fifty dollars be resarved to purchase a Horse for Fanny or
Rebecca-- and be it understood that any property my daughter
Betsey may receive agreeable to this will is to be intailed to
her and the heirs of her Body. and my will is that at my wifes
Decease my plantation shall be Eaqualy divided according to
quantity and quality betwixt my Sons -- and all the other
property that may then belong to my Estate in any way or manner
that is not otherwise disposed of by this will Shall be Eaqua-
lly divided among my Children then living

And I do hereby Constitute, make, and appoint Susannah Hill
and Thos. Willson the sole Executor of this my Last Will and
Testament, Revoking and Makeing void all others In witness
whereof I have hereunto set my hand and Seal this fifteenth
day of Octr. in the year of our Lord Eighteen Hundred and
twelve

Signed Sealed and pronounced by the Sd. John Hill as his
last will and Testament in the presence of us who in his presence and in the presence of each other have hereunto Subscrib
ed our Names.
Dudley Mabrey
Samuel Rosamond
Saml. Hill

his
John X Hill (SEAL)
mark

WILL OF JOHN HILL JR.

In the Name of God Amen. I John Hill Being of Sound and Dis-
posing mind & memory but weak in body and Calling to mind the
uncertainty of life and being Desirous to Dispose of all Such
worldly Estate as it hath pleased God to Bless me with, do make

and ordain this my last will in manner following that is to say
I first Desire so much of my property be sold as will pay all
my just debts, I then will unto my mother Susannah Hill My
negro fellow Gabriel During her life time, or widowhood at her
death or marriage I will my negro Fellow Gabriel Sold and the
money aft ?ag divided between my three Brothers Samuel Hill
Bluford Hill, Joseph Hill and my sister Rebecca Hodges. I also
will and bequeath all the Balance of my Estate, both Real and
personal to the above mentioned Samuel Hill, Joseph Hill
Bluford Hill and Rebecca Hodges to them and their heirs forever.
I also appoint Ruben Hodges, Samuel Hill & Wm Barmore my law
ful Executors

John Hill

Signed and Acknowledged in the presence of us this third of
August one thousand Eight Hundred and twenty four.

Richard A Hodges
William Hodges
Wm Barmore

ANOTHER PAPER.

Stated that   Cogburn & Joicey his wife, David Vines &
Sally his wife, Benjamin Rosamond Jr., Saml. Rosamond Jr.,
Saml. Rosamond Sr. & Fanny his wife, Reuben Hodges & Rebecca
his wife, Patrick Jermain, Thomas Jermain were residing out of
the state. (Note by P.Y. Am not positive of the name Jermain
this name was'nt plain.)

. . . .

ESTATE OF JOHN ALGIER PACK. 3376
BILL TO FORECLOSE MORTGAGE
CLERK OF COURTS OFFICE, ABBEVILLE, S.C.

The State of South Carolina
Abbeville District) In Equity.
To the Honorable the Chancellors of the said State.
     Humbly complaining showeth unto your Honors your orator
Samuel Smith as follows. On the fourteenth day of August in the
year of our Lord one thousand eight hundred and forty one, your
orator sold and conveyed to John Algier a tract of land situated
in Abbeville District aforesaid, then owned by your orator, con
taining two hundred and eight acres more or less, lying on the
waters of long Cane Creek bounded by lands Wesley C. Norwood,
Thomas J. Roberts John Calvert and lands formerly owned by
William Robertson and James Lomax. The said John Algier on the
day aforesaid in payment of the purchase money for the said
tract gave to your orator his two promissory notes, bearing date
the day & year aforesaid, one for the sum of four hundred dollars payable on or before the first of January A.D. 1843, the
other for the sum of four hundred & fifty six Dollars payable
on or before the first day of January A.D. one thousand eight
eight hundred and fourty four, all which by reference to copies

of the said notes herewith filed. And further to secure the
payment of the said notes, the said John Algier on the afore
said fourteenth day of August 1841 made and delivered to your
orator a mortgage of the said tract of land, bearing com date
the conveyance from your orator to the said John Algier & with
the notes aforesaid, which mortgage does not contain any dis-
tinct or plain reference to the notes aforesaid but recites
that it is given to secure the payment to your orator of the
sums of money specified in the said notes and at the times
therein limited.

And your orator will ever pray &c.

                                              Perrin
Filed 10 March 1843.   Compts. Sol.

. . . .

                 ESTATE OF THOMAS KIRKPATRICK PACK. 503
                 PETITION FOR GUARDIAN
                 CLERK OF COURTS OFFICE, ABBEVILLE, S.C.

The State of South Carolina
Abbeville District) To wit.
To the Honorable the Chancellors of said State.
     The Humble Petition of Margaret Kirkpatrick Respectfully
Sheweth. That Thomas Kirkpatrick her father lately departed
this life intestate seized and possessed of a considerable
estate real and personal, and leaving amongst other distribut-
ives of his estate your Petitioner who is entitled to a share
or portion thereof. Your Petitioner is now twelve years of age,
and desires that her mother Jane Kirkpatrick be appointed her
guardian.
     Your Petitioner therefore prays that her mother Jane Kirk-
patrick be appointed her guardian, and invested with the right
of such appointment.
     And your petitioner will ever pray &c.
Test   her
Thomas Thomson   Margaret X Kirkpatrick
                                    mark
I consent to be guardian of my daughter Margaret Kirkpatrick.
9th June 1851.   Jane Kirkpatrick

         . . . .

                 ESTATE OF MARTHA A. WIDEMAN PACK. 503
                 PETITION FOR GUARDIAN
                 CLERK OF COURTS OFFICE, ABBEVILLE, S.C.

The State of South Carolina
Abbeville District) In Equity.
To the Honorable the Chancellors of the said State.
     The Humble Petition of Martha A. Wideman Respectfully shew
eth that she is a minor over the age of choice to wit about
sixteen years old. That she is entitled to aconsiderable
Estate which has descended to her from her father Leonard

Wideman late of Abbeville District, now deceased. She there
fore prays that James H. Wideman her brother may be appointed
her guardian and vested with all the powers and duties of such.
     And in duty bound she will ever pray &c.
                                    Martha A Wideman

I, Sarah Wideman mother of Martha A Wideman do hereby relinq-
uish the guardianship of my said daughter, and consent that
James H. Wideman may be appointed the guardian.
Abbeville
17 Jany. 1849   Sarah Wideman

. . . .

NOW IN COMPILATION

OLD PENDLETON DISTRICT RECORDS, ANDERSON COURTHOUSE.
VOL. 1. MEMOGRAPHED . 50 PAGES PLUS CROSS INDEX. PRICE $5.00.

OLD 96 AND ABBEVILLE EQUITY RECORDS. VOL. 2 . MEMOGRAPHED.
50 PAGES PLUS CROSS INDEX. $5.00.

COMPILED AND PUBLISHED BY THE PAULINE YOUNG GENEALOGICAL
SOCIETY, BOX 129, LIBERTY, S.C.

CALHOUN, WILLIAM HENRY 74
JOSEPH 2

CALVERT, JOHN 98

CAMPBELL, WILLIAM 66

CARTER, ALEXANDER 28

CARTLEDGE, ELIZABETH 29

CHILES, NIMROD 62-63
FERREY 62
SUSAN 62
ELIZA 62
LUCINDA 62
JOHN 64
WALTER 63
MILTON 70
MARTHA 70

CLARKE, COL. ELIJAH 2
JOHN 85

CLAY, S.H. 75
ELIZA 75

COCHRAN, D.H. 49
JOHN 68

COLLIER, EDWARD 55

COOPER 14
JAMES 53

COMPTON? THOMAS M. 73

COGBURN, JOICEY 95

COX, ROBERT 64

CRAWFORD, JOHN A. 73

CRESWELL, THOMAS 55
JOSEPH SR. 52

CUNNINGHAM, COL. 43

DARBY, BASDAL 47
MARTHA 48

DAVIS, ROBERT 50

DEPOSITER, JOHN C. 92

DERRICOTT, R. 56
DEVLIN, JOHN 48

DODSON, JAMES 95
JANE 95

DOOLEY, GEORGE 4

DONALDSON, MATTHEW 77

EDGEFIELD DISTRICT 57

EVANS, DANIEL 28

FITCHETT, DANIEL T. 46

FLORIDA, SUMTER CO. 75
SUMTERVILLE 75

FOSTER, JOHN 47

FRAZARS CREEK 47

GEORGIA, JASPER CO. 64
JONES CO. 92
HENRY CO. 92
LINCOLN CO. 92
FAYETTE CO. 92
WAYNESBORO 28
ELBERT CO. 44
RICHLAND CO. 44
WILKES CO. 1
RICHMOND CO. 21
BURKE CO. 28
CASS CO. 73
ST. GEORGES PARISH 44

GERMAIN? JOICEY 95
PATRICK 95
THOMAS 95

GIBERT? JEREMIAH T. 71

GIFT, JONATHAN 30

GILLESPIE, ANDREW 71

GLASGOW, SAMUEL 53

GOLDING, REUBEN 62
SUSANNAH 62
GOODWIN, JAMES 55

GRAHAM, ELIAS 88
CAROLINE 88
WILLIAM SR. 88
JOHN 95
ELIZABETH 95

McKELLAR,	JOHN SR.	80
	JOHN W.	80
	JAMES D.	80
McMILLION,	THOMAS	47
MABREY,	JAMES F.	75
	CAROLINE ??	75
	REUBEN L.	76
	DUDLEY	97
MARTIN,	JACOB	70
	ALEXANDER	68
	JOHN A.S.	57
	CHARLES	57
	THOMAS P.	57
	JOHN C.	58
	JACOB	69
	WILLIE B.	69
	NANCY	69
	GEORGE W.	70
	MARTHA	70
	ROSENNA E.A.	70
	NEOLINA	70
	JOHN B.	70
MATTHEWS,	JOHN	1
	ISAAC	42
MATHIS,	PATIENCE	28
MAYS,	MATTHEW	88
	LARKIN	88
	HENRY	88
	ELIZABETH	88
	SARAH	88
	CAROLINE	88
	LUCRETIA	88
	MEDY JR.	88
	NANCY	89-95
	LARKIN	89
	DANIEL	89
	JANE	89
	ABNEY	89
	TELITHA	89
	WILLIAM	95
MAYSON,	ARCHEY	62-64
	JOHN C.	64
	CHARLES	80
MEEK,	CAROLINE	75
	ROBERT D.	75
MEYERS,	MICHAEL	81
	SALLY	81
	LEONARD	82
	JOHN	82
	GRACE	82
	ELIZABETH	82
	DAVID	82
	JONATHAN	82-86
	CATHARINE	82
	BETSEY	87

MILLER,	GEORGE A.	66
MISSISSIPPI,	PONTOTOC CO.	4C
	PONTOTOC CO.	74
	HOLMES CO.	75
MITCHELL,	T.	53
MORGAN,	E.C.	47
MOORE,	JOHN	56
	JEMIMA	56
	THOMAS LEWIS	56
	HEREMIAH EDWIN	56
	JNO SINGLETON	56
	MARCUS D.	47
	CATHARINE	45
MORRAH,	HUGH	89-90
	SARAH	89
	JANE CAROLINE	89
	MARY 91-	89
	ELEANOR 91-	89
	ROBERT	90
	JOHN	91
	SAMUEL	91
	DAVID	91
	JANE	91
	GEORGE	91
	SARAH	91
MULBERRY	CREEK	89
NAIL,	CASPER SR.	82
	CASPER JR.	82
	DANIEL SR.	87
NOBLE,	PATRICK	91
NORMAN,	JESSE	93
NORRIS,	ROBERT	47
NORTON,	JULIUS	46
NORWOOD,	WESLEY C. 98-	91
NUSON,	SOLOMON	39
O'MARGY,	ROBERT	68
OUSBURN,	THOMAS	47
PAGE?	ROBERT	45
PAIN,	MR.	43
PATTERSON,	JOSIAH C.	53-65
	ROBERT S.	65
	MARY D.	65
	JAS. NAPOLEON	65
	ROBT. LEWIS	65
	NANCY	65
PAUL,	WILLIAM P.	46
PETTIGREW,	MR.	41
PERRY,	ISAAC	28
PHILLIPS,	MISSES	89
PICKENS,	GENERAL	30
PINCKNEY,	THOMAS	7
POPE,	HENRY N.	93
POPE?	ROBERT	45
PORTER,	HUGH	48-49
	WILLISON F.B.	49

McKELLAR,	JOHN SR.	80
	JOHN W.	80
	JAMES D.	80
McMILLION,	THOMAS	47
MABREY,	JAMES F.	75
	CAROLINE M.	75
	REUBEN L.	76
	DUDLEY	97
MARTIN,	JACOB	70
	ALEXANDER	68
	JOHN A.S.	57
	CHARLES	57
	THOMAS P.	57
	JOHN C.	58
	JACOB	69
	WILLIE B.	69
	NANCY	69
	GEORGE W.	70
	MARTHA	70
	ROSENNA F.A.	70
	ANDELIRA	70
	JOHN S.	70
MATTHEWS,	JOHN	1
	ISAAC	42
MATHIS,	PATIENCE	28
MAYS,	MATTHEW	88
	LARKIN	88
	HENRY	88
	ELIZABETH	88
	SARAH	88
	CAROLINE	88
	LUCRETIA	88
	MEDY JR.	88
	NANCY	89 -95
	LARKIN	89
	DANIEL	89
	JANE	89
	ABNEY	89
	TELITHA	89
	WILLIAM	95
MAYSON,	ARCHEY	62-64
	JOHN C.	64
	CHARLES	00
MEEK,	CAROLINE	75
	ROBERT D.	75
MEYERS,	MICHAEL	81
	SALLY	81
	LEONARD	82
	JOHN	82
	GRACE	82
	ELIZABETH	82
	DAVID	82
	JONATHAN	82-86
	CATHARINE	82
	BETSEY	87

MILLER,	GEORGE A.	66
MISSISSIPPI,	PONTOTOC CO.	48
	PONTOTOC CO.	74
	HOLMES CO.	75
MITCHELL,	T.	53
MORGAN,	E.C.	47
MOORE,	JOHN	56
	JEMIMA	56
	THOMAS LEWIS	56
	HEREMIAH EDWIN	56
	JNO SINGLETON	56
	MARCUS D.	47
	CATHARINE	45
MONRAH,	HUGH	89-90
	SARAH	89
	JANE CAROLINE	89
	MARY 91-	89
	ELEANOR 91-	89
	ROBERT	90
	JOHN	91
	SAMUEL	91
	DAVID	91
	JANE	91
	GEORGE	91
	SARAH	91
MULBERRY	CREEK	89
NAIL,	CASPER SR.	82
	CASPER JR.	82
	DANIEL SR.	87
NOBLE,	PATRICK	91
NORMAN,	JESSE	93
NORRIS,	ROBERT	47
NORTON,	JULIUS	46
NORWOOD,	WESLEY C. 98-	91
NUSON,	SOLOMON	39
O'MARGY,	ROBERT	68
OUSBURN,	THOMAS	47
PAGE?	ROBERT	45
PAIN,	MR.	43
PATTERSON,	JOSIAH C.	53-65
	ROBERT S.	65
	MARY D.	65
	JAS. NAPOLEON	65
	ROBT. LEWIS	65
	NANCY	65
PAUL,	WILLIAM P.	46
PETTIGREW,	MR.	41
PERRY,	ISAAC	28
PHILLIPS,	MISSES	89
PICKENS,	GENERAL	30
PINCKNEY,	THOMAS	7
POPE,	HENRY N.	93
POPE?	ROBERT	45
PORTER,	HUGH	48-49
	WILLISON F.B.	49

PRESSLY,	DAVID	53-68
	JOHN	62
	PERRY	62
	ELIZA	69
	EBENEZER E.	69
PRIOR,	JOHN	81
	SALLY	81
PRINCE,	EDWARD SR.	58
	EDWARD JR.	58
	LUCY	58
	HUDSON	59
	JOSEPH	59
PRUITT,	LEVI	39
QUARTER	CREEK	72
RAINEY,	POLLY	95
	JESSE	95
RED,	SAMUEL	2
REES,	HUGH	39
RAIGUNS,	JESSE	68
RICHEY,	ROBERT C.	95
	NANCY	95
RICHARDSON,	SARAH	91
	JOHN	91
ROBERTS,	THOMAS J.	98
ROSAMOND,	THOMAS	88-95
	BENJAMIN	89
	SARAH	88
	JAMES	95
	SAMUEL	95
	JOHN	95
	JOSEPH	95
	WILLIAM	95
	FANNY	95
ROBERTSON,	JOHN	50
RUTLEDGE,	HUGH	1
SALUDA	RIVER	89-72 -64
SAMPLE,	ALEXANDER	71
SANDERS,	JOSEPH H.	45
	JOHN	45
	FRANCES	45
	CATHARINE	45
	REBECCA	45
SAVAGE,	JOHN	85
SAVANNAH		87
SAVANNAH	RIVER	55-56-14-61
SCOTLAND		80
SCOTT,	JOHN	51
	THOMAS	51
	ELIZA	51
	SAMUEL	57
SHARP,	JOHNSON H.	89
	CAROLINE	89
SHINHOLDER,	WILLIAM	87
SMITH,	ROBERT SR.	65
	SAMUEL	98

SPRINGLE,	FRANCES	45
	WILLIAM	46
STARK,	WILLIAM L.	93
STEPHENS,	JOHN	50
	MARY M.	50
	SARAH JANE	50
STEWART,		40
	WILLIAM	54-62
	ELIZABETH	62
	ALEXANDER	72
	PEGGY	72
	M.T.	91
STRICKLAND,	ELI	93
TAYLOR,	MAJOR	44
TARRENS,	JOHN	39
TENNENT,	MRS.	47
TUCKER,	WILLIAM	61
	ETHEL	61
TWIGGS,	GENERAL	30
WARDLEWORTH,	SAMUEL	64
WARDLAW,	JAMES ESQ.	46-77
WATTS,	SAMUEL L.	47
	BEAUFORT T.	65-87
	JOHN P.	65
WATERS,	JOHN ESQ.	89
WEEMS,	JOHN W.	73
WEATHERS,	EDWARD	28
WHITLEY,	STEPHEN	88
	ELIZABETH	88
WIDEMAN,	MARTHA A.	99
	LEONARD	99
	SARAH	99
WILLIAMS,	W. C. & J.E.	75
WILLIAMSON,	McALISTER	91
WILLINGHAM,	ISAAC SR.	92
	ISAAC JR.	92
WILSONS,	CREEK	51
	JOHN H.	74
	JOHN S.	94
	SUSAN	94
WIMBISH,	WILLIAM	93
WILSON,	SIBBY	72
	DRURY	72
WOOLDRIDGE,	JOHN	60
	THOMAS	60
	BETSEY	60
	FRANCES	60
	MATILDA	60
	LUCY	60
	NANCY	60
	WILLIAM	60
	SUSANNAH	60
	SALLY	60
	HARRIET	60
	PATSEY	60

WRIGHT,   MICHAEL   83

VINES,   SALLY   95
            DAVID   95
            NELIA   96

YARBROUGH, JOHN F.   67
            JOHN W.   67
            SARAH   68
            HARRIET C. 68
            RICHARD S. 68
            JAMES M.   68
            MARCELLA E. 68

YOUNG,   SAMUEL   53-72
            JOHN   53
            MARY   52

www.ingramcontent.com/pod-product-compliance
Lightning Source LLC
Chambersburg PA
CBHW072150020426
42334CB00018B/1941